JoAnn L. Steinbach
901 16th Street
Granite Falls, MN 56241

C0-BWZ-993

AGAINST ALL ODDS

A Child's Trials and Tribulations

by

Ron Fulghum

DORRANCE PUBLISHING CO., INC.
PITTSBURGH, PENNSYLVANIA 15222

The contents of this work including, but not limited to, the accuracy of events, people, and places depicted; opinions expressed; permission to use previously published materials included; and any advice given or actions advocated are solely the responsibility of the author, who assumes all liability for said work and indemnifies the publisher against any claims stemming from publication of the work.

All Rights Reserved
Copyright © 2006 by Ron Fulghum
No part of this book may be reproduced or transmitted
in any form or by any means, electronic or mechanical,
including photocopying, recording, or by any information
storage and retrieval system without permission in
writing from the publisher.

ISBN-10: 0-8059-6994-2
ISBN-13: 978-0-8059-6994-8
Printed in the United States of America

First Printing

For information or to order additional books, please write:
Dorrance Publishing Co., Inc.
701 Smithfield Street, Third Floor
Pittsburgh, Pennsylvania 15222
U.S.A.
1-800-788-7654
Or visit our website and online catalogue at www.dorrancebookstore.com

Disclaimer

The opinions expressed herein are not necessarily those of the publisher.

Cover Credit
Maggie O'Neill
O'Neill Studios LLC
1855 Calvert St., #201
NW Washington D.C. 20009
(202) 265-2888
www.oneillstudios.com

This is a story about two boys, twins to be exact, brought into this world fifty years ago. There was no family in their lives, no one for guidance or support. What these young boys would discover was this—if you haven't family or friends to guide you, life can be as hard and dangerous as a steep winding road, with harm and peril lurking at every turn. It didn't take long for them to discover the road of life that lay ahead would be very difficult. The choices they would make, from the simplest to the most difficult, would prepare them for a journey that would bring them much pain and suffering. One thing was for certain—with each decision they made would come knowledge and understanding. They would discover this to be the truest barometer for learning the toughest test of life! Would they be able to endure the countless trials and tribulations life would bring? Or would they crumble under its weight?

These young boys would soon discover they could trust only their instincts for survival in life. They soon realized their friends would become enemies. They were unprepared to endure against a world looking to devour anything representing meekness and innocence. These young boys would discover they needed to become men very early and very quick. Perhaps not as seasoned or disciplined as a man, but a man nonetheless!

Each day would bring new events. The hardest were the ones where they had to choose whom to listen to and whom to disregard. It was always a hit-and-miss proposition, where the winner and the loser were the same. With each struggle they had to endure constant questions without relevant answers.

God didn't prepare these boys for this type of journey, nor did God prepare anyone else for that matter. However, these young boys learned to reach out to someone they couldn't see, but always suspected was there, to guide them or perhaps pick them up when they fell, or help heal a wound when they struggled and lost in their decision-making.

• • •

In preparing to write this book, I considered there would be some who might question my sincerity and my memory. My answer for those doubters is this—I can remember as far back in my memory as the age of two years old. I'm haunted by these memories. It's as if each memory happened yesterday. I remember vividly because the bad events of my youth reach out to me, trying to pull me back, as if trying to devour me. My writing this book is an attempt to rid myself of these awful memories and perhaps to help others who have suffered through similar events as I.

CHAPTER 1

Our young lads were brought into this world in a small town in Tennessee. I will refrain from giving exact names and places. This way our story will be a fairy tale, open for anyone's interpretation. If we allow those who read this story to reach into the darkest part of their mind and rediscover places and events in their lives where each has had similar moments, perhaps they will discover and understand a little of what these children endured. One of the boys became the leader. From the very beginning he was tolerant and understanding of life and where he and his brother always stood. He didn't fully understand everything he saw, but he was blessed with some magical insight that prepared his judgment for making the decisions which were best for him and his brother.

When these two boys were brought forth into the world, it was truly a mistake. The two adults, if you could call them that, weren't capable or willing to assume the responsibility of raising children. You might say it was in the heat of passion the brothers were conceived and delivered into life. After their birth this moment of passion would become nothing more than a distant memory, something they wouldn't experience again until they became adults.

Ready or not, they came into life and breathed their first breath. If life had been merciful, the angel of death would have come and delivered them from the persecution they were certain to endure! However, somewhere a higher power seemed to intercede and let them breathe on, and ultimately thrive, in an environment filled with hate and anguish. It soon became apparent that neither of these adults could be responsible for raising these two miracles, let alone feed them the nourishment of life they would need and crave...knowledge and love.

For the next two years the two boys were constantly neglected and pushed aside, until their mother couldn't bear the responsibility any longer and gave them to the state. She told the authorities she was unable to care for them, but in reality she never wanted to accept responsibility for raising her sons. So the two boys became wards of the state at the tender age of two. It's a shame I can't remember the earlier years. Perhaps I'm lucky though. I'm regretful that everything I remember from my early childhood contains nothing more than hardship and remorse.

For those who are reading and wondering why this mother gave her children to the state, you aren't alone. I have constantly struggled with this and wondered the same thought. Throughout my life, I haven't gone a day where I've looked at my own children as they grew and thought to myself—only death with its cruel, cold embrace would pry me from their lives. Until my final days, when I pass on to whatever exists for us after we die, I will await the answer from a heavenly father, who perhaps will enlighten me when I ask one question—"Why did she give us life, then leave us to die?"

For those who have known parents in their lives and received reassurance, love, and affection, imagine these two boys who are now wards of the state. There is neither love, affection, caring, or holding. In all the years I was under the state's care, I can't remember being held or told the most tender and caring of words—"I love you." This, my friends, is the cruelest fact of life—to be brought forth as a miracle of life, then to have no one to hold or share those words of love and say they care for you.

Don't get me wrong, the state did care, but it wasn't the care and nutriment that children are raised by. There were people to answer to if those responsible for raising us didn't care, but it was the house-parents who were given the responsibility to give us direction and make us "toe the mark," something I will elaborate on later on in this book.

Our first stop in life was a children's home, on top of a little mountain in Tennessee. I haven't a clue if it's open today. If it is, so be it, but from my experience there, I could care less. Places such as this exist only for the purpose to put children in a place where there are three square meals provided each day, and a roof over their head. There wasn't anything good or creative about the way we were raised. I thought this was how life was everywhere. Boy was I wrong.

We became little slaves of the state. We cooked, cleaned, and did the state's bidding until we outgrew their arrangements. If we were lucky, we might be adopted. If not, we would remain within the confines of the institution, or be sent to the next children's home to be developed and raised as the state saw fit.

At this first home, my brother and I were too young to know right from wrong, so as you might expect, we were in trouble most of the time. We weren't mean or outrageous. We were just discovering what little boys were about, and sometimes we got into trouble, as happens with any child. However, when you get into trouble within the state's jurisdiction, there's a price to pay. Let's just say that when we screwed up and were punished, it didn't matter if you were two or twenty-two. You didn't make the same mistake twice.

I remember one particular incident when we were given grilled cheese sandwiches for lunch. I wasn't particularly fond of them, but when the state feeds you, there isn't a choice, like in a family environment, so you eat what the state feeds you. In this particular instance, I didn't like the sandwich. It was greasy and cold, but if I went back through the lunch line to drop off my tray, I would be punished for returning it. The state always made it very clear that we were never to waste anything. To avoid being punished, I did what most children would do. I hid it. I took the sandwich to my room and put it under my pillow. Wrong move. I forgot about it. The next day when the beds were changed the housemother discovered it.

Do you know what happens when you place a greasy sandwich under a pillow? Grease spreads everywhere! The pillow and the sheets were ruined, to say nothing of the mattress. I was punished and made to sleep on the floor for two weeks. It was December. The winter storms were hitting us hard on that mountain. As you might expect, the floor was frigid and I caught a bad cold. Our housemother, to save face, and to keep from getting into trouble with her boss, told her supervisor I was running around outside without a jacket. When I tried to let them know it was a lie, I was slapped in the face for talking back!

For those who haven't been slapped before, let me explain something. I was four years old, very small and very frail, so this very large adult saw fit to correct me. The way she thought to correct me was to slap me hard. I remember crying for some time. When I was told to stop crying and didn't, I was slapped again. I remember my ear ringing for some time after this first incident.

Earlier I mentioned the judgments and decisions I would make that would be filled with pain and suffering. This was lesson number one. I wasn't slapped again after this first incident, except in anger. You might say I learned the hard way. However, for me it was my first lesson in life, that projected me to become someone who learned to hate. It would clearly help me in the future.

Every Sunday, my brother and I would watch groups of adults come and go. At first we didn't understand what was happening, but as little ones we had many ways to discover what was happening We asked the other children what was going on. To our surprise, we learned that parents would come on every Sunday to visit their children. We were stupid and naive to think perhaps someday our parents might come.

I hope I haven't lost any of you, but there were some children in these homes who were there simply because they didn't mind their parents. The state would place these kids in these homes with the hope they would come to their senses, grow out of their mean streak, and go home. Some did, some didn't. My brother and I weren't one of the fortunate children to be adopted. We were eligible for adoption, but the state had one requirement—if you wanted to adopt one of us you had to take the other. The state, in their infinite wisdom, would not let us be separated. For those of you who are thinking that surely there were some families who wanted a set of twins, think again. If there were, they stayed away from our school. We never saw or experienced anyone wanting to adopt us until much later in our lives. I'm getting ahead of myself; I need to settle down and get back to my story.

Every Sunday, for the next five years, my brother and I would go to the end of the drive, sit on the sidewalk, and watch the cars come and go. The official visitation period was only for five hours, and that's where we devoted our time each Sunday, hoping someone would come to visit us. In all of those years, in all types of weather, and in every imaginable period, no one ever came. My brother and I became fixated by the single thought that there had to be someone out there who cared, who wanted to see us and be with us. But it never happened.

My brother and I were in this first state home for five years, until we reached the age of seven. Not one person ever came to visit us. Remember when I said the decisions I would make for my brother and I would be the most profound and important decisions I would make? When I finally realized there wasn't anyone coming, I looked at my brother, put my arm around him, and told him it was over, and we had to move on. I told him we were by ourselves, and we needed to look after ourselves. This was a huge turning point in my life. It was at the tender age of seven, I accepted the responsibility of raising and looking after my brother. I felt it was my responsibility after what we had gone through in the early years. I knew it was for the best. I could trust him and he could trust me. From that point on, we wouldn't ever trust another adult until much later in our teenage years. I sometimes wondered if we were the only ones alone in this screwed up mess.

In the visitation periods, we witnessed special events where we saw other children celebrating birthdays with their loved ones. When the state takes a child and accepts the responsibility of raising that child, their birthday was the last thing the state ever thought about. I can't remember much about our birthdays. I didn't think much about them. To me they were just another day, nothing to make a fuss about. I didn't know my own birthday until I was in the third grade. Then it struck me why the other kids were given special gifts and things. I never understood, until I asked about it later. When I found out, I wished I'd never asked. I had to tell my brother. For the first time in my life, I saw him cry. It was something I wouldn't forget and I would get used to seeing him cry plenty. For both of us, it was sometimes too much to bear. Who in this world would ever do this to any child and not hold themselves responsible for these cowardly acts? I had come to make another profound decision in my life—I wouldn't let my brother's birthday pass without giving him something special. I didn't have any money, but if I couldn't buy him something, I would give him my dessert or something he liked. It never mattered what I gave. The simplest of things—candy, my dinner, my good shoes or a favorite shirt—it was the act that counted, and with that I established another important lesson and objective in my young life. It was always the intent of giving that mattered most to me, not what I gave. My greatest reward for many of my early years was the joy of seeing my brother smile, and knowing I had made his day special. I learned at a very young age in life, what some adults never learn. The simplest of things are sometimes the most rewarding. Simply giving of yourself, and not thinking about anything but giving your very best, is the greatest gift of all.

Our lives weren't always filled with dismay and grief. Sometimes it got pretty exciting. I told you about the winter storms we were experiencing on top of that mountain. Well, there was this particularly rough one where we experienced

4

a strong ice storm. It was so bad that when it finally stopped snowing and sleeting, we had eighteen inches of ice all over the mountain. Every power line was down and a huge pine tree fell through the boiler room, breaking a steam line causing us to lose our heating source.

Being up on this mountain, stranded with no heat and power, everyone had to improvise to conserve heat and water. The superintendent of the school gathered all of the older girls and requested them to sleep with the younger boys and the older boys were requested to sleep with the younger girls in the gym. This way everyone had a partner to huddle with at night to keep warm.

To pass time we played games by pulling blankets across the gym floor and sliding around on the floor. Those were the fun times. The bad times were when it got really cold, about ten to fifteen degrees below zero, and the water would freeze. We didn't have anything to drink, and things got bad quick.

My brother and I were assigned to sleep with this tall older girl named Cheryl. I believe she had a very profound impact in my life. It was nothing sexual; we were only six years old. I was held and kept warm by someone other than my brother. I couldn't remember being held by my own mom. When my brother would cry at night, this girl would comfort him and tell him everything was going to be all right. This girl, who had never before ever befriended us until this moment, was teaching me something about life. I had never before seen compassion. Cheryl would kiss my brother on the forehead, sing to him, rock him to sleep, and let him know there was someone out there that cared! I really got confused and I had to ask some very difficult, and from my perspective, some very stupid questions. I didn't understand. I didn't know or realize what was transpiring before my eyes. I was seeing gentleness for the first time I could remember. I was experiencing firsthand something many books are written about, the simplest form of love there is. Something neither my brother or I had ever experienced. Cheryl would later become my friend, and would explain emotional things about compassion and understanding, something that I've carried with me to this very day. It was something the state never taught me in all those years I was under their direction. Now, you're probably asking yourself, just how long was I under the state's direction? Until I graduated from high school at eighteen—sixteen long years!

When the storm let up, the superintendent finally got his two-way radio working. He was an old radio buff, and he figured the storm was preventing anyone from acknowledging his signal. Nor could he receive anyone's transmission. When he did get it working he contacted the state authorities and let them know the damage we suffered. In the next four hours, the National Guard, under the direction of the governor, sent a convoy of half-tracks up that mountain with more than eighteen inches of ice on the roads to get us off that God-forsaken piece of rock. When we heard those half-tracks coming up the road, it sounded like music to our ears. The soldiers brought sausage biscuits and hot chocolate. It was the first thing we had eaten in two days. Anything would have been good for a group of hungry children.

5

We were a cold, weary bunch. The National Guard Engineers couldn't restore heat and power, so they began to load us up and truck us off that mountain. If you've never ridden a half-track before, going down a mountain road with eighteen inches of ice on the road is unthinkable. Every now and then, our truck would slip and slide a bit until its tracks dug in and found a firm grip. This wasn't for the faint of heart, and it really wasn't for the strong of heart either. It took us more than five hours of slipping and sliding to get down that mountain. At the bottom were more than one hundred families waiting and ready to take us into their homes, until they could repair the damage to our school.

I don't remember exactly what transpired over the next two weeks. However, I discovered something about home life, up close and personal. It's different, strange, and downright bewildering at times. We weren't accustomed to anything like this. When you're brought up in a state institution, with no parents to speak of, then suddenly thrust into a caring, loving environment…it's shocking to say the least. Suddenly, we were surrounded by adults who weren't screaming at us at the top of their lungs and were somewhat pleasant to be around. It was strange and yet different. Even more, it was confusing. Why? We were being raised by a state-assigned house parent, removed from a harsh, unbending environment, and thrust into a home where we were asked what we would like to eat. Was there anything they could do for us? And what would we like to do? These were questions that had never, up until that moment in our lives, been asked of us before. Were we taken aback, confused? You bet your…. Yes, we were confused, and at the same time enlightened. Did we take advantage of the situation? Hmmmmm, what do you think? We loved every single moment.

The family that took my brother and I in was an elderly couple who never had children. They reveled in the fact they could spend some of their precious time to devote themselves to a couple of young boys, and perhaps make the next two weeks of our lives seem like a little piece of heaven. And heaven it was. For the next few weeks we were fed as much as we wanted and whatever we wanted. We really thought we had died and gone to heaven, but do you know what was more precious to us? It was the mere fact that every night before we went to bed, this couple would come into our room together and read us a short story to bring us peace and comfort. For those of you out there who have never experienced this, it might not seem like a big deal, but it was to us. I'm an observer of life, and I've learned more from watching others than any book could ever teach me. What I was watching and learning now, I taught to my children many years later. I didn't forget that special feeling I received and what it meant for me to have someone give of themselves as this couple had given to us. They didn't know us, but they gave from their heart, the way we're all supposed to.

We were in heaven. We didn't want this to end. We were cared for and protected for the first time in our life, and we absolutely loved it. However, all good things must come to an end and they did. Just short of two weeks, the couple received a phone call from the state authorities. They were told that the next day someone from the school would be coming by to pick us up. When we were told the news, I noticed a tear in the eyes of the of the elderly lady who had taken care of us, as if we were her own. I kept on asking myself, "Why?" What possible good could come of this? The couple tried to make things comfortable for us, but for the first time in my life I became attached to someone. I didn't understand the situation and I didn't want it to end.

The next day, like clockwork, the state came by and this couple, whom I never saw again, wept bitterly as we were escorted to the bus to take us back to our former home. They weren't the only ones crying that day. You might say it was another lesson learned—never get attached or take anything for granted, because when you least expect it, and especially when you aren't ready for it, you receive that revolting jolt to your senses, and you're shocked back into reality.

I never forgot those dear and warm people There are times I wonder what became of them, and why they never came to see us at the school. I hope someone, somewhere, recognized the love and effort they gave to my brother and me! They surely deserved the opportunity to have other children, but I can't dwell on that.

Upon returning to our home on the mountain, the place was a shambles. It needed repairs and cleaning badly. Pipes were broken and it seemed everything that worked before the storm didn't work at all now. There would be lots of work to do before this place was home again.

My brother and I settled in, trying to make light of everything we had learned, and trying to rekindle friendships with those who had befriended us during the storm. But something strange happened. When things were desperate, and we were all in dire straits, people change. Now that things were back to normal, people's lives were back to normal. The last thing they wanted was a couple of snotty, young, inquisitive boys interfering with their lives. Another lesson learned. No one at school seemed to care much about anyone or anything, other than themselves and their own little precious world. I would understand why in time. It was strange to see why these children could at one point be so kind and caring, and now withdrawn and completely closed-minded. I should have known better; however you might say the love and affection I received at the temporary home my brother and I stayed in made me somewhat complacent.

Over the next few weeks, and many more months to follow, my brother and I discovered we had really lucked out staying with the people we were assigned to. Some of the other children weren't as lucky as we were. Some were beaten, neglected, and sexually abused. Remember Cheryl, who took care of my brother and I when the storm hit? She was placed with an obese couple. The man raped her repeatedly over the next two weeks. She was told if she tried to tell the authorities from our school, she was told that if she said anything, it would simply be her word against his. He told her he knew where she lived and would make her pay! This kind, warm, young girl was abused by a system that didn't care and wouldn't do anything to help her. As you will see later, this wouldn't be the first time I discovered these facts. It not only happened to the girls, but the boys as well. In fact, to the very person who is telling this story!

7

It took me a long time to understand exactly what happened to me. I'm certain that children, no matter what age they are, shouldn't ever experience things like this. I thought for the longest period that I was the one at fault.

What happened to me wasn't pleasant. It's always difficult to open up the dark closets within our mind and bring forth events, no matter how tragic or painful they might be, so bear with me. We, as human beings have developed a subconscious reflex to subdue those thoughts we abhor the most and file them away where we hope they may never resurface. I promised myself when I started writing this book, I would be perfectly honest with myself, even when I knew it would involve opening up these portals in my memory and bringing back memories of some of the pain.

I'm more structured today than I was then. I was only a child, I've come to realize. I did nothing wrong. I also realize I was a victim and nothing more. Every child wants to feel they belong. I was no different. I wanted to be loved, but not like this. I wondered if anyone would or could love me. I honestly didn't know. I had a hard enough time getting people to like me, I couldn't imagine anyone loving me. It seemed it wasn't to be for me!

The winter storms came and went. It always seemed we were getting hit by something. If not heavy snow, it was ice or sleet. We didn't get to play outside very much, so we did what every kid does to pass time we played or made up games. We weren't at liberty to watch television, because it wasn't very popular with the state. Only the house parents had televisions to watch, and believe me, they didn't want us around on their off hours, sitting by and watching television. There were always some who got to watch, but not very many.

There was this older boy at our school. Everyone seemed to look up to him, and it seemed everyone was afraid of him. The danger flag in my subconscious should've gone up when he approached me. However, I was distraught over coming back from the couple who took care of my brother and I after the winter storm, I was looking for a friend. His approach to me was somewhat candid and reserved. Being a little boy I had absolutely no idea what was on his mind. I should've known better, but sometimes the greatest lessons we learn from life are the bitter ones. I didn't know what was on his mind and I didn't care. He was a friend of my own gender. I welcomed it, as anyone who didn't have many friends would. Gradually he brought me into his confidence, and asked me to come to his room for some candy. This is where the bells and whistles should've gone off. They didn't.

Let me stop here and explain something to you. I was a young boy who, up until that point, didn't have two cents to my name, much less any way to earn money for candy. Here was this boy offering me candy, so I strung along, fascinated by the fact it was free for the taking. Little did I know, it wasn't free and I was to learn it would cost me plenty. This boy, who we'll call Joe, lured me to his room and closed the door. Nothing seemed wrong, but I became very nervous and concerned. I didn't like the situation. I felt if I tried anything he might get angry and do something which would really hurt me, so I tried to be as calm as I knew how. It didn't take long before I knew he had plans for me and I knew I was in real trouble.

Without going into great detail, he had his way with me and threatened that if I ever told anyone about what happened, he would kill me! I was frightened and terrified about what happened. When he finally opened the door, I bolted down the hall and ran for my room as fast as my little legs could carry me. All I could remember as I ran was his laughter in the background. I cried myself to sleep that night. For the longest time, after that evening, I considered taking my own life.

You're probably asking yourself—how could this little boy consider something as drastic as that? I was only seven; what did I know about suicide? Wrong again. You have no idea, absolutely no idea what goes on in these schools. From the time I was knowledgeable, and intelligent enough to tell time, I'd seen more kids try to take their own life, because of emotional problems, abuse, neglect, or simply dying from lack of love. They couldn't go on with the life they were given. I was scared. I wasn't happy with the thoughts of what had happened. It scared me terribly, and I couldn't deal with the thought of going through something like that ever again. I became another victim, someone who was looking for friendship, and found hardship and trauma instead!

Children are some of the most resourceful people I've ever come to know. It has never ceased to amaze me what they could come up with if the situation was important enough. I've seen girls overdose on aspirin, drugs, even Drano simply because they were hurting and couldn't go through something as demoralizing as what they had suffered ever again. I never condemned them from where I sat. I simply stood by and wondered—when and if the time came for me, when I knew I'd had enough, what would I do? Would I have enough guts to do what needed to be done? I wasn't as certain as they were!

You should also understand what our minds were going through. We were children; we were being abused right and left by anyone who saw the need or was perverted enough to force their will on us. I never saw one child, boy or girl, who sought to be abused. The abuse came looking for us. When it found us, we had nowhere to run and no one to go to for help. You do the math. What would you do in our situation? We did what each of us felt we had to do to remove the pain. Sometimes it was a bitter pill to swallow; however you always knew when you heard screaming and crying, someone, somewhere, had had enough and they sought to end their pain. I was very fortunate and lucky I didn't have the guts. I was tough enough to install a mental block and open a black door in the darkest part of my mind and place this event in my life and close and lock the door. It would be some thirty years later before I would unlock that door and finally rid myself of these vilest of thoughts. I would also have my revenge on Joe. But that is another part of the story.

We all have a cross to bear at one point or another. It was always a constant reminder to watch, look, listen, and learn from the events and the hardships around you. I did, and that is why I am writing this story today. Some of the other children weren't as resourceful. They sought other ways to bury their pain!

9

Life went on as usual around my brother and I. We kept mostly to ourselves, tried to stay out of everyone's way, do whatever we were told, listen and try to learn. Sometimes we were successful, but other times we weren't. It was in those times we learned what vengeful wrath was all about. Have you ever seen an adult that lost their temper and struck out at anyone available to ease the anger and hatred in their minds? I have and it isn't pretty! Many of the kids in our school had scars—I'm not talking about mental scars either! Sometimes the beatings got so bad that bones were broken, cuts were inflicted, and wounds were opened. The thirst to release their anger on us was sometimes more than even they could bear. We saw it as just another punishment, but when things got out of hand and the house parents started using fists and sticks, we knew it was more than just punishment.

Throughout everything I remember about our younger years, I've tried to remember the good along with the bad in order to maintain some perspective about our life. We were no different from any other children our age. We didn't have parents or family who wanted us, but we were children with imaginations, and with our imaginations we were able to conjure up thoughts and ideas of what we thought family life was supposed to be like. My brother and I would play games where we'd take turns acting like fathers and pretend to teach our children what was right and wrong. It was times like these where I was most thankful, for in play I could escape the hardship I knew would come each night when we had to go to bed and hear many of the children cry themselves to sleep, because they were lost in despair and wanted the pain and hurt to go away.

I remember those long and lonely nights when I would hear my brother cry. I would go to him, crawl into his bed to talk to him and let him know I was there. This simplest of expressions came with great risk. The house mothers had rules about one or more boys being in bed together. Even though we were brothers, it didn't matter. When I was caught, I paid a price. Sometimes I was ready to pay, but other times I wasn't, because the punishment wouldn't always be the same. Sometimes it was worse for giving kindness to someone and being with my brother to bring him a small measure of comfort and reassurance.

My brother and I didn't always abide by the state's wishes. There were times when we thought we'd come to the end of our rope and we would try and run away, to get away from the loneliness and hurt. Somewhere in our little minds, we thought there had to be someone, somewhere we could go and find happiness. Remember that elderly couple we were sent to after that winter storm? We always tried to go back to them. We never made it, but we tried.

I remember one particular time when we ran away. We were walking down the mountain, holding each other's hand and carrying our belongings in a little bag. We didn't have much, and we would look for someone to give us a ride—anywhere, it didn't matter where. Well, this particular time, we were perhaps three or four miles from school. We were looking for a ride and a car came up to us and stopped. There was a lady inside, and she asked us where we were going. In the best lie I could muster, I told her we were going home, and our parents had forgotten us at the gas station when they stopped to fill up. She offered us a ride, so we got in. *This is so simple,* I thought to myself. We were on our way. Little did I know, this lady who seemed so nice had turned around and was taking us back to school and the home on the mountain. We were so small we couldn't see out the door, nor did we have a sense of direction about where we were going. When she stopped the car and told us we were there, I was so happy. Imagine my surprise when we opened the door, and the first thing I saw was the superintendent walking up to us with anger in his eyes. He asked us where we thought we were going, and he told us to go to our room. He would be there later to punish us.

I don't ever remember being so scared. When he came to our room he brought our house mother, and we proceeded to get the whooping of our lives! It was during this moment in my life, I found something about my hatred and my feelings for these adults around me. I hated them so much that I could channel the hatred into a mental block in my mind, where I could take myself away from the beating I was receiving, and put my mind into a place somewhere far away, where there wasn't any pain. In many ways it was like a trance. I would just stare straight ahead and let them do what they were doing. I neither cried nor moved. When the house mother saw I wasn't crying, it made her furious and she beat me even harder. It was then I discovered unconsciousness. If you can understand a little boy of seven getting beat until he is unconscious then waking up in a medical room and hearing the house mother explain to the nurse that I was doing something stupid in the hall, fell down, and knocked myself out, then you can understand, I hurt. It was then I was thankful for my strange gift. It would cost me plenty in pain, but it was worth it not to let our house mother break my spirit! No one ever did during my younger years; however my spirit would be tested later in life. But that is later.

It was a few days later, when I returned to my room with my brother and he explained to me what had happened to me. He explained how angry our house mother had gotten, how she had slammed me up against the wall in order to try and make me cry. My head hit the solid concrete wall and you might guess what gave first. Exactly, my head. A few weeks later my brother and I were brought to the children's state welfare office in Chattanooga, Tennessee, where the state addressed our mother about our future. We stood there and heard her painful explanations as to why she didn't want us in her life. I heard and understood then—Jon and I were unwanted, especially when you hear from your own mother, in her own words, "I simply don't want them. I don't want them in my life."

I remember looking at my mother when she said those words to the children's welfare officer. With tears running down my face, I realized, I was alone, unwanted, and feeling totally helpless and bewildered. It was then I began hardening my heart and my life for what lay ahead. I would never look back, never again!

One thing I learned during this early period was that the world we were living in only respected the strong. If you weren't strong enough to endure the constant trials and tribulations the world subjected you to, you would most certainly be consumed and spit out as nothing more than refuse. This, I found, was even more pronounced with the other children we were raised with. They would, if

11

they could, on a daily basis take advantage of you, if they thought they could get away with it. So I had to learn these lessons quick, if I was to understand when those around me were trying to take advantage of my brother and I. I had to harden myself to the belief, "trust no one but yourself first," and make everyone else prove themselves. By doing this, it helped lessen the pain if you had your eyes open to others' true intent. There were times I failed miserably, but there were other moments when my insight and better judgment saved us from some pretty serious consequences.

CHAPTER 2

Life wasn't always hard for my brother and I. We always found things to amuse ourselves and fill our days! We didn't have many toys to speak of. When you live in a state institution, you find they really don't waste a lot of money on toys and things to interest children. So my brother and I would improvise, as little boys do when they have constructive imaginations. We would find anything and everything we could and invent things to do. One of the things we loved to do was float little bottles down a creek and look for salamanders. One day my brother and I were playing with a stick and trying to hit a little rubber ball. We didn't know it at the time, but this was a game children played all the time in Philadelphia called stickball. It wasn't much, but we had fun at it! We were always into something, and we tried as best we could to consume the time we had each day with things that made us happy. It broke the boredom, and certainly helped us deal with the realization that we were alone and things would only be as we would allow them to be.

13

Think of our situation as this—we were raised in a place and time where television wasn't exactly a heavy and open commodity. The radio was to everyone something of magic and wonder, but we didn't have a radio, so we would do just about anything—and I do mean anything—our little imaginations could think of to have fun. Mud was a favorite, however not for our house parents. When they saw us, we would get scolded, then rushed to the showers and forced to clean up. Then, to our dismay we would get punished for having fun. A strange life, but one that we had to endure.

We would do anything to have friends; however most of the kids in our school had cliques, as any school does, and my brother and I were too young to belong or fit into their social order. Although my days of not fitting in made me better, as you will discover later in this story, not belonging in any clique or group made me self-reliant. I didn't want to ask anyone for anything. It simply was me and my brother and what was most important to us, our happiness. Keeping that was a full-time job, even for a child.

It was always hard each Sunday to see other parents come and go and see other children laughing and happy with their parents or loved ones. It always hurt. Don't ask why, it just did. My brother and I would always watch from a distance. We had to, because we found out on numerous occasions that other parents didn't like to be watched. They would shoo us away! When this happened, I would take my brother to the ball field and throw a ball or just sit and talk. This happened more that I care to remember. It wasn't our fault we didn't have anyone. Sometimes we felt as if we were to blame for the loneliness we felt!

You're probably asking yourself, what did we talk about? Think about it—you were a child once, what did you talk about when you were a child? You daydreamed a lot and we were no different. Children talk about the most insignificant things sometimes and we were no different. However one general subject which always came to the forefront was what we'd do when we grew up and what we might do if the situation were reversed. We always had hope, and sometimes hope is all you need to get you through a tough situation. Believe me, we had our share of tough situations.

I always seemed to be out in left field, playing the game of life without a glove. Playing a game that I didn't know but wanted desperately to understand. Sometimes life is like that, and you have to make the most of it as life allows you to grow. I used to think if I went one day without learning something, it was a wasted day. In our situation, I didn't have that luxury, and it always amazed me that I seemed to always learn one thing or another, even if it was a tough lesson filled with pain.

Every time my brother and I would go off by ourselves, I believed we were constructing a little world all to ourselves. It seemed to grow alive each time we would sit and talk. I believe the little things we discussed on those lonely days helped construct for us the future and the difficult period that lay ahead. We talked about having parents, being parents, what we would do, and the mistakes we wouldn't make were the roles ever reversed. These little insignificant discussions lay the groundwork for the hard days ahead for us when we would become parents. The promises we made on those lonely days weren't promises without merit or structure, and they had more value than you could ever understand. Let me explain.

One day we were sitting and observing a group of children and their parents. At least I think they were their parents, but something seemed strange. These two kids and their parents were having a good time, laughing and playing, when all of a sudden I saw the father reach over and slap the crap out of one of the children. This shocked me. It was also very frightening how the chain of events played out. The man just starting whaling away on this little boy, who couldn't have been more than eight or nine years old. Here he was, one moment laughing, the next moment crying his eyes out and getting slapped around. I didn't learn until later that the little boy had said something in jest; his father took offense to it and let him know about it! What I learned from that incident was to stay away from that monster whenever he came back to visit, but the most important thing was to listen constructively.

What I saw from this perspective, and this particular incident was that our views weren't always the same, and if you allow yourself to do three simple things, you'll learn and grow. What are those three things I'm speaking of? Stop, Look, and most importantly, Listen! If you allow yourself to perform these three things on a consistent basis you'd be surprised how much insight can be gained. You also have to remember I had to perform these important items each and every day. It was how I learned good from bad. Sometimes I learned things well, other times I didn't. You will hear about these later.

I witnessed events in my life every day that amazed me and always seemed to bewilder me, because I simply had no insight as to what I had seen. I certainly didn't always understand. I wasn't dense, but I was trying to learn. It was frustrating sometimes. What am I referring to? Let me explain again.

The game of life doesn't come with a rule book, especially for a child, which is what I was. It was difficult, even if I could read, and I still didn't understand. It would take many examples for me to learn what was right and what was wrong with every situation. For example, when we talked to an adult, there weren't any explicit rules on the proper ways to speak to them. I learned many times, that every adult, no matter who or what level of importance they held in life, was different. The most difficult factor to learn was that each and every adult I had to face, seemed to change their personal perspective each and every day. Talk about confusing and frustrating. You could say one thing one day that was okay, but the next day, I could say the same thing—and get my head knocked off. I was always taught to say, "yes ma'am" and "no ma'am," to end a question to a lady, and "yes sir" and "no sir" to a man. Depending on the situation and the perspective of a particular adult, you noticed I didn't say our house mother was or wasn't a lady. Believe me, she was far from it. This situation would or wouldn't suffice and I would get creamed!

I learned to use the three words I spoke of earlier very wisely. If I didn't know the correct answer, then I wouldn't say anything at all. Even this wasn't too bright sometimes, and I had to fall back and regroup when this tactic didn't work. Every day was a learning, listening, and watching experience. Sometimes life is just that way. If you watch long enough, you'll start learning how to fill in the missing pieces to the puzzle. I didn't like puzzles at all, but that is life, the largest and most difficult puzzle of them all.

Once, my brother and I were playing jacks in our dormitory hallway. We were giggling, having fun, and enjoying the moment. Our house mother walked by and for some strange reason, she was having a bad day, and hearing our laugher made it worse for her. I don't know if it was our laughter or us having fun that set her off, but she laid into us and beat us out of the building, yelling at us to stay out until she called us back inside. I was listening, sometime later that evening, well after dark, when she came out, started yelling at us again, and asking us why we were outside after our bedtime. The worst thing we could say—you're correct in your thinking of what our response was to her. After she got through with us, I learned another valuable lesson in life. Sometimes when you're told something, it isn't exactly what was intended. You have to use a certain amount of creative thinking and discretion. Lesson learned. It didn't happen again for some time, but it certainly was different and creative.

Life was always up and down for my brother and me. We learned very early in life to roll with the punches and not to take everything very seriously or for granted. Now that last statement was easier to say than it was to do. Let me explain. Every day we would get up and assume the routine that existed for us at school. First, we had breakfast, then we cleaned our rooms, and then we went to school. Nothing difficult about that, right? Wrong. We weren't the only ones at this school. I learned at an early age that if you want a place in life, sometimes you have to fight for it. Now imagine thirty to forty boys, in one wing of a dormitory, all of them having the same idea at the same time and only a short time to complete everything. It gave new meaning to the term "Chinese fire drill!" I was amazed to see how everyone functioned, trying to wash their faces, comb their hair, brush their teeth, and go to the restroom all in the space of thirty minutes, with only six sinks to use in our wing. You always had fights when someone bigger didn't want to wait his turn and they would wade in, take a sink, and shove whomever was using it aside.

The fights were always brief; however they left a lasting effect on those who were on the losing end of things. That said, guess who always came out on the losing end of that stick? You got it. With my brother and I being every bit of forty pounds and very small, we just lost out. However, that wasn't the real problem. If you were late, and it seemed we always were, you were punished by having to do more work or duty time after school. This got to be a real pain. We tried to explain, but we were told to shut up, get in line, and the house parent would tell us they would take care of us later. They never forgot. It was like clockwork. We would walk back to our dorm, through the door, and our house parent would call us over and describe to us what our punishment was to be. It didn't matter if we'd had a great day; this would spoil everything. They didn't care, and it was their way of letting us know who was boss!

We had our ups and downs as everyone seemed to, only ours had a different meaning and a different outcome. We were so used to getting in trouble, that we finally started volunteering to do anything and everything, just to think we weren't in trouble but doing things on our own.

This worked for a while, but soon we would get into more trouble, and our house parent would really come down on us and give us a spanking. For anyone who might not understand, this spanking isn't what you think. When our house parent gave us a spanking, it was something you never forgot.

Back in those days, it was okay to spank, hit, slap, or beat the kids, as long as no one witnessed our house parents doing it. So as you might expect, when our punishment came down, we could expect anything, and I do mean anything. I remember one particular incident when I was getting spanked. I had closed my mind to the pain I knew was coming by placing my thoughts elsewhere, when suddenly I was brought to my senses by this mother of all pains! I suddenly became aware I was floating, then I came down, hit hard, and the sudden intense pain made me scream. Our house parent, to my dismay, was trying to make me cry and I wasn't. She lost it and picked me up by one arm. Remember, I weighed about forty pounds and was very frail. She started slapping me about the face and head. One particular blow came across my left ear. She ruptured my eardrum. This was something I couldn't do to anyone, especially a child. I remember wailing like a banshee, the pain was unbearable. When I passed out from the pain it got much worse!

When I came to in the infirmary, I was relieved to see the superintendent; however he was listening to our house parent explain her side of the incident and he was listening very intently. One thing that amazes me to this day is that they didn't ask me my side of the story. They loaded me up and took me to the hospital for an examination and found my eardrum was ruptured. However, the doctor was observant in a way I'd never understood before. This man asked me my side of the story, and when I didn't speak, he saw something in my eyes. I didn't know it at the time, but fear was showing in my face. I felt threatened. I knew if I said anything, I would pay dearly. The doctor asked everyone to leave the room. He asked me again. When I didn't speak, he asked me if I was afraid, and I nodded my head up and down, but never spoke. He then told me that he knew that my injury didn't match the house parent's story because he could see the imprint of the house parent's hand on my left ear. He asked me again if someone hit me. For me to not say something at this point in my life would have had some dire consequences, so I took a leap of faith. I wanted this pain to stop, so I told him everything I could remember. Now you're probably thinking that things got better, right? Wrong again. They got much worse for my brother and me.

This doctor whom I took into confidence caused quite a stir when he went off. When I say he went off, I mean he erupted like a wounded rhino. He started screaming, yelling, and went after the superintendent. This, as you might guess, had some disastrous effects. First, when the doctor explained that he would have the super's job, and he was going to the authorities about the incident to correct things, guess what happened? Where do you think I had to go back to that evening? Back on top of that mountain. All the way back up I got an ear full of what was going to happen to me when he got me back to school for causing all this trouble. I was telling the truth and where did it get me? In hot water. Once again, I learned not to trust an adult. It hadn't worked, so what do you think I did? I gathered up everything I owned, stuffed it into a bag, grabbed my brother, and ran from the school and the trouble I knew was to come. I didn't want to get hurt again and I thought it was the best thing I could do at the time.

I always had a great sense of direction, and this time I was certain I wasn't going to let us get caught. Now, getting off that mountain in the dark is quite a trip. During this period there was only one passable road up to our school, and in order to walk off the mountain we would need to perform our great escape in the dark. We had a full moon to navigate by, and the cold night air was something we could endure. We were also blessed with a helpful sign if anyone was coming our way. The cars of that period were absolutely deafening and you could hear someone coming from a long distance.

My brother and I started out from the school around ten in the evening, and we made good time moving down the main road from the school to the main highway. Every time we heard a car coming, and before the lights from any vehicle would shine on us, we would get off the road, crouch in the ditch that ran alongside, or hide behind bushes that were within three to four feet from the road's edge. We were making good time. Things seemed to be going in our favor when we heard a vehicle coming down the road. My first thought was that it couldn't be anyone from the school; however they were driving slower than normal traffic, as if they were looking for something or someone. I grabbed my brother and I pulled him into the bushes deeper than we had gone previously. I knew something was up and I wasn't about to get caught just yet! As the car approached, I noticed the people inside were shining a large flashlight into the bushes. As they approached, I told my brother to lay down flat on the ground and not move. The car was moving slower now, and they were only twenty to thirty yards from us. If you could have had a hand on my little heart, you would have felt it beating about a thousand beats a minute. Was I scared? You bet your sweet...I was terrified of the thought of being caught and having to answer to our house mother.

My left ear still smarted plenty, and I didn't want to get hurt again, so I sucked it up and tried to be as still as possible. The car was only a few yards away, and I told my brother not to breathe so no one in the car could see our breath in the night air. Why I said that, I have absolutely no idea, but you know what? It worked. The car was now passing by us, and I could see the reflection of the superintendent in the passenger window. How did I know it was our superintendent? He always wore a large hat, and this shadow I was watching slowly pass us by had a large hat on his head. You think about that and I'll get back to our story.

My brother and I waited about ten minutes, when we heard the car turn around and go back up the road. We came out of the bushes, looked up the road in the direction the car had gone, and we ran as fast as our little legs could carry us.

There are times in life that running as fast as you can isn't fast enough. Sometimes you have to run faster when you're in the trouble we were. You'll find, as I did, that it can be pretty darn fast.

My brother and I ran for about ten or fifteen minutes until we thought it was safe. Our only thought was to make as much distance as we could between us, the school, and that car, and to do it as fast as possible. Besides, I knew they were possibly thinking we couldn't have gotten this far. They were wrong, big time.

All my life, I knew I had a gift for running. Not particularly fast, but for long stretches, and now I was trying to make the most of that ability. My brother was tired, but I urged him to keep the pace. I was holding his hand and pulling him with me. We made great time. Exactly how well I'll never know, because we didn't know how to tell time. All I knew was we had to move, and brother and sister, did we move!

As we ran down the road, I became aware the downward slope of the mountain road had evened off, and we were now in the valley below the mountain. I thought we were safe and we could slow down, at least for a little while. We walked side by side, not knowing where we were going, but knowing we didn't want to go back to that awful school.

We must have been tired. We had covered a lot of ground. I didn't notice the sound of a car coming down the road. I should have, but didn't. Before I knew it, I heard a voice yell out, "Hold it right there!" I slowly turned around to see this cop getting out of his car before it stopped. He was on the passenger side; he was a very big man and to tell you the truth, I was tired. I knew I couldn't out run him, so I stood there and let him grab me. His first words were like a bullhorn going off in my ear. Remember I had a sore left ear, I was hurting, and I wasn't aware of how bad I felt. He yelled again and asked us where in the Sam hill we thought we were going? I thought to myself that it was a pretty good question; however I didn't know where we were and I didn't really know exactly what to say. So I stood there looking up at this big man and shrugged my shoulders. He looked at me and my brother and asked us our names. I told him we were Ron and Jon. He asked if we were from the school on the mountain. I said yes. Why, you might ask? I didn't have any idea what he was going to do with us. I knew I didn't want to get hurt again, and if I lied, I thought he might slap me, so I told the truth. He told us the school had called and said to be on the lookout for two runaways that were identical twins. They thought we were dead. I knew we were in serious trouble now.

The big cop led us over to his car and motioned for us to get in the back seat. The big car slowly rolled off the side of the road and moved up the roadway. Then something strange happened. This big cop, who yelled at us to stop, turned around and offered my brother and me a sandwich. Then he started asking us questions about why we were running away.

Folks, I have no idea why I said what I did, but I told the cop exactly what happened to me. I told him about all the events that had taken place. You'll never guess what happened next. I realized this big cop was listening to me. I didn't believe it at first; however when the car stopped, and the driver turned around and started asking us questions, I knew I had an audience.

Sometimes honesty is the best policy. Sometimes it isn't. This time it was. When we finished our story the big cop asked me just where we thought we were going. I told him as firmly, and with all the conviction I could muster, that we'd go anywhere we could, as long as we didn't get hurt again. The big cop did something then that was strange to me. He asked me to lean forward, looked at my left ear, which was still swollen, and he asked me if it hurt. I told him it did. He slowly turned to his partner and told me, without looking at me, that if he could do anything, he would make sure no one ever hurt us again, as long as we were with

19

him. He said something to me that no one had ever said to me in my short life. He said, "Son, everything's going to be all right." I didn't even know what "son" meant, but believe me, I was a very quick study.

The two cops took us back to the police station. They led us inside the station, and let me tell you, I was scared. My brother was crying, because everywhere we looked we saw cops. It seemed the further we got into the building, the more cops we saw. I have no idea what happened, but it seemed that everywhere we looked, everyone had their eyes on us. They looked mad for some reason. I thought they were mad at us, so I just looked down at the floor and slowly stopped walking. Something really weird happened then. All of a sudden, one cop after another came up to us and asked us if we wanted something to drink, ice cream, candy, or a sandwich. At first it was really strange, and then it dawned on me— these cops were slowly learning about what happened to us. They weren't mad at us, they were upset with the school—in fact they were downright mad about it.

We'd been in the station for about an hour, when the superintendent from our school came through the door. Upon seeing us, he yelled at us, saying, "You boys are going to pay now!" Guess what happened? The big cop, who told us in the car we wouldn't get hurt again, stepped in front of the angry super and asked him if he condoned what happened to us? The super made the worst mistake of his life. He said yes. The big cop suddenly got even larger, and with friends. His fellow officers gathered around him and told the super he was under arrest for what had happened to us and it was he who was in big trouble now!

To make the story short and simple, the super lost his job and was fired by the state. Jon and I were relocated to another home, where we would begin the next chapter of our lives. We didn't see that big cop again, but I didn't forget him. I have always looked on our law enforcement personnel in a special way since that day, for the special way we were treated. They gave me something new in my life— hope! I knew if these people cared about me, then perhaps there was happiness out there somewhere for us. We just had to keep on searching and not give up.

CHAPTER 3

I've always been a show-me kind of guy. If you want to teach me anything in life, please show me first. I will learn more from that small example than I will from anything else you might provide. I've learned from small but simple examples. If you listen and learn from the little things, the big things won't hurt as much, and they might even be a tad easier. Remember, in our world, everything my brother and I were exposed to seemed to revolve around pain!

The next place for my brother and I was easier in many ways, but the level of difficulty was a notch higher. This place didn't have any fences or guards, and we were allowed to go to public school. Now for all of you laypeople out there, many state institutions have schools on the campuses where the children were housed. Why? For this simple reason—to keep their problems out of the public eye and enable themselves to do whatever they wished. The state loved to keep things out of public view.

We were housed in dormitories where some forty-five to sixty children lived and slept in a single wing. This didn't allow much for privacy, and it didn't allow much for hiding things you wanted to keep private and to yourself. You had to develop thick skin. If you didn't, the other boys would get on you and ride you pretty rough.

We had one boy at our school that was the bully type. He loved to show everyone how tough he was. When we were on campus he was okay, just another boy. However, when he got to school, it seemed the devil came out in him. Being new to the school, my brother and I tried to fit in and behave. However, this kid thought we were weak and he saw another chance to prove his toughness. One day in class, he came up to my brother, punched him dead in the face, and hurt him bad. I wasn't there at the time, but when I heard about it, I ran to the nurse's room to check on him. Jon had a busted nose and he was bleeding badly. I discovered something about myself then. I had a controllable temper.

What does that mean? It means I wanted some payback and would accept anything to get my measure of revenge. It took about three days before I would get my chance; however this boy thought he'd gotten away with hurting my brother. He came into my classroom, walked up behind me, and punched me in the back of the head. Folks, it hurt. Real bad. However, when he yelled at me to do something, I stood up, looked him right in the eye and told him, not now, but at recess. He laughed at me, as did everyone else in class. Big mistake. I didn't have much going in my life, but I did have my pride. I waited until class was over, and when the bell rang I calmly got up, walked out the door to the playground, and waited for this kid to come to me. I knew he would and when he did, you know what happened? He walked up to me and started to say something, but before he could, I took my right hand and I shoved it up his nose as hard as I could! Folks, that punch was a punch heard 'round the world. I broke his nose. He started bellowing like a wounded rhino. I'd never seen so much blood! One of the teachers ran up to me when he saw all the commotion, grabbed me, and said I was in big trouble. However, all of the kids spoke up and told the teacher the other kid started it, and I was only defending myself.

That kid never bothered my brother or I after that. You might say I gained a lot of respect from him and others, as well as a reputation. If you bothered one of the twins, especially me, you would pay, so it was best to leave us alone. They did. I wasn't a fighter, and never have been, but I had my limit! This would help me in future years. I don't condone violence, but I certainly don't run from a fight. I discovered you can't allow violence to control your life. There are always stronger, faster, and meaner people in the world, and if you choose this path of life and allow it to control you, it will surely consume you and spit you out.

My brother and I tried to fit in at the school. We soon discovered something new about life that we hadn't really noticed before—girls. We were now about ten years old, and we were discovering that girls were something to be admired. At first I didn't notice, but my brother sure did. He got a fancy about this young pretty thing. He got all goo-goo eyed and everything. Now when I say goo-goo eyed, that's exactly what I mean! Every time she passed by us in the cafeteria, my brother would see her and simply go limp. I am extremely happy that I didn't get this way until I was about sixteen years old. So I had to sit back, watch with dismay, and learn the hard way. I did learn the hard way—very hard!

My brother starting talking with this girl and got to be very good friends with her. They always seemed to be together. Her initials were C. M. and if she ever reads this book, she should know he never forgot her and would have followed her to the end of the earth. Which is exactly what might have happened, if I'd let him. However, one day she let him know she was being adopted and would be leaving school in a week or so. This struck my brother like a sledgehammer. He was devastated. He had really gotten to know and love this little girl and it was tearing him apart to see her go.

The day she said goodbye to Jon, and got into the car to go to the airport, was the sickest day my brother ever had. He didn't eat for about a week after she left school. He was really down, and he started getting into trouble. He was headed downhill with no purpose at all. I simply didn't know what to do. Something happened one day that would tear him away from me. It would take a part of my brother from me that I would never see again.

Jon got into a bad fight one day with a much bigger kid. You might say it was almost a case of suicide. I never discovered what started it. This kid hurt my brother real bad. He spent about three weeks in a hospital from the beating he took. When he returned to school from the hospital, I knew he had changed, I somehow sensed he wasn't the same person I'd always known.

One day he came up to me and out of nowhere he told me he was leaving school and running away. I asked him where he was going. He said he was headed for California. I asked why. "To be with C.M.," he replied. I couldn't stop him. Later that night, Jon started out of our cafeteria on his way back to the dormitory. Standing there on the sidewalk was the boy who put him in the hospital. Jon walked by him, when all of a sudden the boy stuck out his leg and tripped him. I'll never know why, probably just pure meanness. What happened next was as vicious a beating as I've ever seen. This boy started whaling on him again for no reason. The other boys knew I would go to his aid and they grabbed me. I was held there helpless, as I watched this kid, about fifty pounds heavier than my brother, beat him into unconsciousness.

When a couple of matrons finally stopped the beating and pulled the boy off my brother, all I could see was blood. I have no idea what caused it or why but I knew it would never happen again if I had anything to do with it. There are many things in life I despise, and one is those who hurt the weak. This boy was now at the top of my list. In time, he would receive his just reward—if not from me, then from someone else. However, I hoped to get to him first!

Incidents like these are constant reminders to me today about where I was in life then, and where I am now. They aren't pleasant memories, and they serve as a constant reminder to me of what the bad times could be like. I fight the memories constantly to keep them from consuming me from the true realities of this world and the ever-present struggle we go through to simply exist within this violent world.

My brother was taken off campus to a hospital, where he remained for about six weeks. It was until much later that I learned he'd almost died. He had his face beaten in, and it was broken in about seven places. Upon his return to school, his attitude and demeanor was nothing like what I remembered before the attack. He wasn't the sweet innocent brother I once knew. His whole demeanor was different, and he didn't care about anything. He had no purpose, he was bound for destruction, and he simply didn't care. Life changes you when you receive a beating like he got. Anyone who says it doesn't should change places with him for a day or a week. They'll find they are terribly wrong!

I did everything I could to keep Jon happy and to try and find the little brother I had once known. It was until much later that I realized the brother I once knew would never return. His innocence was destroyed and gone forever. I would

23

never forgive the state or the boy who hurt him. Jon went his own way for a while, and I knew we would have to make some changes. It wasn't safe for him here, and I wasn't going to allow anyone to hurt him again if I could help it.

There might be some of you who are asking what happened to the kid who almost killed my brother. Let's just say that I have a long memory. I would get my revenge and he would pay dearly, but that would come some six years later. However, the present wasn't the place nor the time to gather my revenge. But when the time came, it would be sweet and decisive as lightning striking a tree. The state transferred the kid to a detention unit for about two years, but he only got worse! He would be transferred out of state to try and help him with his problems. That trip didn't help either.

My brother got worse. When you receive a life-threatening beating not once, but twice, it changes you, physically and mentally. He wanted to fight everything and everyone, including me. I always took the whooping he gave me and would ball up and let him beat on me. I couldn't hit him after what I'd seen him go through, so I took his beatings and tried to make up afterwards. It would work, and for a while he returned to normal, as the brother I'd always known. However, later events would change that and caused me to lose him forever.

There was one matron at our school who had previously served as a prison guard before he was given his present position. You're probably thinking to yourself that is crazy. Why would the state hire a former prison guard to watch and raise children? My point exactly! Anyway, one day my brother and I were out in the hall, playing in front of the cafeteria. This guard came out with a bullwhip and started whipping my brother and me. We started screaming and crying. One of the female cooks came out, saw what was going on, and went back into the kitchen. She grabbed a big cast iron skillet and beat him off us; however the damage was done, and she was too late. One of the blows the matron struck hit my brother between the legs. Jon was ruptured and bleeding. He was rushed to emergency surgery and, once again, almost died.

Now I found hatred, sheer dark hatred, as an ally that would help me survive the rest of my days. I discovered if I couldn't solve or control my thoughts, I could learn to hate as never before. If the state would allow someone as precious as my brother to be beaten time and again and simply allow it to continue, then I would take matters into my own hands. My brother would be beaten only twice more in my lifetime, which I will inform you of later. Now back to our story!

My brother was in the hospital for three weeks. Upon his return, I had already thought of what I was going to do, and my plan was set. I wasn't the one to get the worse of the beating, but I was going to give the worst in return! When my brother returned, I waited until his strength returned. When you go through something like he did, you lose a lot of weight and stamina. When he was strong enough, I would strike!

We waited for about three weeks, and then one night we called our matron into the bunk area. Now if you think this is strange, think about this—that criminal was still on campus watching over the kids. The state never removed him,

24

even after the investigation. Sick, isn't it? Well if they wouldn't, we would find our own way! We called him into the bunk area. When he entered, some of the larger boys grabbed him. They tied him to a column, where my brother and I beat the living crap out of him! Then we ran from school. Not as cowards, mind you. We ran to make sure no one could harm my brother again. When I looked back, the other boys in our bunk were having their turn with him. After this, the state finally reacted and did something. However, it was the kids who sealed his fate. As far as I knew he would never raise a hand to hurt another child. Never!

My brother and I were gone from the school for about three weeks. We were caught in Florida and were returned to Tennessee. The state didn't know what to do with us. They put us in a detention unit for about nine months until they could make up their minds. We had no idea how long we would remain there; however we knew we weren't going back where we came from. The state made sure of that!

Do you have any idea what a detention unit is? Let me tell you, it's just like a prison, only this one is for children. The type of kids you find there are those who don't listen, don't mind, and are destructive to others around them. Just your every-day hoodlums, thieves, and malcontents. Did my brother and I deserve to be there? Did we do anything that was so destructive as to justify being detained and locked up every night? Absolutely not, but in the state's infinite wisdom, we did, so here we were until they could make up their mind about what to do with us next.

My brother and I were only eleven years old at the time, and we weren't the destructive type. We certainly weren't a threat to society, but who was going to question the state as to what should or shouldn't be done with children, especially those under their care?

Jon and I were placed together in the same cell to pass the time. We talked about what our next move would be when things changed. Jon was pretty quiet most of the time. He suffered a lot over the course of the past few months. I could only sit there and wonder what was going through his mind. I suspected it wasn't good, but he was my brother, and I would support him in any way I could.

We hadn't been there for more than four months, when we received a visitor. Now folks, hang on to your hats. Our visitor was our mother's brother—our uncle. He had gotten word through the existing channels that Jon and I were in town, so he developed a guilt complex, and thought he would be a better man and come down to visit us. This man came in like he had known us all his life, which he didn't. He couldn't tell us apart and he got our names mixed up every time he addressed us. He told us about our parents, where they were living and what they were doing. To our amazement, he asked if we would like to see them. This is where things got real screwy, and our lives were about to change for the worst. Have you ever heard the expression, "out of the frying pan and into the fire"? That is exactly what was about to happen.

I have no idea how this guy pulled off the things he did. He arranged for us to be allowed to visit our parents for two weeks. Our father was no longer married to our mother. It seemed that during the few years Jon and I were up on that mountain, our father had gotten in trouble with the law. He was arrested and serving thirty years in a chain gang in Tennessee. That's right, a chain gang. In the South, during the fifties and sixties, when the punishment fit the crime, you were sentenced and forced to work your time off working in chain gangs. My father was forced to work his tail off for screwing up in life.

Perhaps the worst part of this story is about to happen. The only good thing I'm about to share with you is that my brother remained free from harm. This time it was to be my turn to be projected into harm's way.

It was strange riding in our uncle's car, going to see someone I couldn't remember. The strangest thought I had was, *What would I say and do?* I hadn't the foggiest idea, and frankly, I didn't care. All I remembered about the moment was going to a place called home. Strange, isn't it? We had to wait eleven years to finally say those memorable words.

It seemed like an eternity for us to get there. Children always ask their parents, "Are we there yet?" when they're excited about going somewhere. We were no exception, and I'm sure we asked that at least a couple hundred times. When we heard the memorable words "We're here" come from our uncle's mouth, I can only tell you how happy we were. Excited and elated were the words. We bolted from the car when he stopped. I can't remember ever being more excited. To finally see our mother was going to be the happiest moment of my life. Or at least I thought it was!

We had to wait for our uncle to come and open the gate, because in our excitement, we couldn't figure out how to open it. When he opened it up, Jon and I rushed to the door. It seemed a little strange when no one came right away, and for good reason. Do you think, in those eleven years, things had changed? Nope, they hadn't at all. Our mother still didn't want us. The whole visit was our uncle's attempt to try and mend some fences, so to speak. He wanted to see if he could get his sister—our mother—to come to her senses, and accept her responsibility as a mother, and raise her children.

She wasn't exactly thrilled, seeing us standing there on her front porch. In fact, she seemed downright upset and perturbed about the whole scene, and she didn't hesitate to let her brother know it either. This is where things got nastier than a rabid bucktooth dog. Our mother laid into him right there on the front steps. She didn't pull any punches or reserve any feelings. She let him know exactly what she felt, with Jon and I standing there, and told him time and again she didn't want us in her life and he shouldn't be sticking his nose into places where he didn't belong. Now, if you're thinking to yourself, what are those boys thinking and feeling at this moment, let me tell you, if I could have found a rock and crawled under it, I would have. I felt as if someone had reached out and punched me in the gut. I was hurt. I looked at my brother, and he was just standing there and looking up with a sad face, not saying a word. It was then that I think we sank to the lowest level of our young lives. We felt absolutely unwanted and alone. Folks, let this be a lesson to you about arguing with your family or friends when children are present. It doesn't exactly help things when you say hurtful comments and let your children know they're not welcome in your life. In the South, as well as other places of the world, we have a name for people like this. It's called trash. I really would like to use another word; however I'm trying to keep this as clean as possible.

We stood there while they yelled and fussed at each other. Then the strangest thing happened. Our uncle, who had brought us to this place, suddenly turned, walked off the porch through the gate, and said as he was getting in the car, "If you don't want them, take them back and address the state yourself; I'm washing myself of the whole affair." If I'd had any common sense at that exact moment, I would've gotten into the car with our uncle and taken my chances with him. However, I never said I was the brightest of kids in the class, so I stood there along with my brother and awaited what might happen next. I guess you know by now that we were feeling pretty low, so what happened next is a complete mystery.

As we were standing there on the porch and listening to those two adults yelling and cussing at each other, you might say they caused quiet a stir. All of our mother's neighbors were standing out on their porch, trying to figure what in the Sam hill was causing all the ruckus and commotion. She had to save face, so she suddenly went in the opposite direction with her emotions. If you thought we were confused before, imagine what we felt like then.

My brother and I had never been held by any adult in our entire lives, except by the elderly couple who took us in when we had the winter storm on the mountain. This wasn't the same, and I knew it instantly. The way she grabbed us hurt, and it wasn't any type of loving, emotional grasp. She downright hurt me, as she ushered us off her front porch and into her living room. You might think that it got better, right? Nope, wrong again. She sat down on her couch, looked at us, and said, "What am I going to do with you two now?" Folks, if you thought I was confused before, what I felt at this moment was downright lost. I always thought I had some sense of judgment in many areas, but for this one I was completely, utterly lost.

She looked at me and my brother and without saying another word, she got up and walked out of the room. Jon and I just stood there, each asking ourselves quietly, unable to speak, what was going to happen next? We didn't have to wait long. Our mother came walking back into the room with not one child, but two. It seemed we weren't the only children in this family. She had gone and had two others with our dad before he got locked up. The plot was thickening, so to speak!

She introduced us to our sisters for the first time. One of the girls was seven, the other was five, and I'm still refraining from using names. In time, I will explain why. We looked at them, and them at us. I thought to myself, *What do we do now?* It was strange to see someone you could finally call family, but they weren't. I didn't know them, and they didn't know us. Strange, to say the least!

I was happy to know Jon and I weren't by ourselves anymore, but also quite sad when I realized our position hadn't changed. The whole reasoning behind our mother not wanting us got even clearer for me. It suddenly dawned on me, the real reason she didn't want us was: we were another two mouths to feed, clothe, and take care of. I didn't fully understand this, and I really didn't care. The facts

27

stood there in front of us. There was no denying it takes twice as much money to take care of four children, especially if you didn't want two of them in the first place.

Not once did she ask us if we wanted anything or ask us if we were hungry. She asked us to go out back and play, and she would call us if she wanted us. It was tough to see someone you held with reverence and pride and finally realize you meant nothing more to them than a problem. I felt about as tall as a snail when it gets stepped on at that moment. I knew things weren't going to get any better, and you'll see they get quite resentful and much worse!

We were outside sitting on the ground, looking at our new sisters. Not many words were coming from either of us. One of our sisters asked us where we came from. I didn't know exactly what to say, so I just shrugged my shoulders and looked at her. The other sister asked Jon who we were, and again, we hadn't a clue so we just sat there and looked at them. Weird, isn't it? To finally see some of your family for the first time, then become speechless. It gets worse.

We were outside sitting and playing, doing what kids do, when we noticed a large car pull up in the driveway. Out of this car came the largest man I'd ever seen in my life. He had this bewildered look on his face. Imagine leaving for work in the morning and coming home to see twice as many kids as you had before. He didn't know exactly who we were; however you might be catching a clue as to the predicament we were in. This man seemed to grow larger and larger as he walked up to us. Imagine the look on his face when he heard one of the girls tell him, "Look Dad, our brothers." I saw a look come across his face that can only be described as sheer terror and shock.

He turned slowly, without saying a word, walked into the house, and yelled out as loud as he could, "Mary! Come here right now!" He started yelling, cussing, and throwing things, saying he wasn't going to stand for this, he wasn't going to stand for that, and so on. All the while, we just sat there with this help-less feeling of utter rejection. You might think things got better, right? You knew they would come to their senses and see things as they were and try to make the best of it, correct? Wrong again. We sat there for what seemed like an eternity and heard all sorts of things, from he wasn't going to feed all these children, to what are we going to do now? If it were left up to me, I would've grabbed my brother and left. If I'd been smart, I would've. However, as I said before, I wasn't exactly the brightest kid in the class.

We were made to go to bed and ride it out for another evening where both adults said they would sleep on it and make a decision the next day. Once again, I should've gotten up that evening and left. As things would play out, it would have been the smartest move of my life.

That night, as we slept, I felt a feeling, as little boys do when they need to go to the bathroom. I got up and walked to where I thought the bathroom door was. I was half asleep as I walked down the hall; however the need to relieve myself was overpowering, so I walked on. I was suddenly met by the man who presum-ably was my stepfather. He asked me where I was going and I told him I had to go. Then he said, "Let me help you!"

This man was about 6'3", and he weighed over three hundred pounds. He opened up the door, picked me up, and threw me inside. At first I didn't know what was going on, then I felt myself falling and falling. Where he had thrown me wasn't the door to the bathroom, but the basement door. I felt like I was flying, until I struck the first landing of the stairs, about ten or twelve feet down. When I hit the first landing, I hit first with my left elbow, breaking it in the socket, the next point of contact was the rear of my head, busting a large gash in the back of my head, which would require twelve stitches to close. In the same moment, I also felt the left side of my ribs strike the railing as I went flying down the second flight of steps. Let me tell you, I now knew what pain my brother endured when he got the crap kicked out of him back at the school.

I have absolutely no idea what made this man do what he did. I certainly wasn't a threat to him, but here I was at the bottom of the basement stairs and hurt. How bad I didn't know, but it was so bad that I slipped into darkness.

I have no idea how long I lay there, unconscious and bleeding. When I awoke, I didn't know where I was, and I didn't know what to do. I couldn't walk, so I crawled up the steps as best I could. I haven't a clue how long it took me to reach the top. When I did, all I remember is crawling down the hall, back in the general direction I thought my brother was sleeping. Upon getting there, I crawled back into bed and lay down. My brother awoke a short time later, hearing me moan and to a feeling that made him assume the bed was wet. It was wet all right, but not from one of us having an accident. The gash in the back of my head was bleeding pretty bad. It had soaked the pillows and sheets. I don't remember much after the screaming stopped. I found out later that I went into shock from trauma and loss of blood. My brother also had to have medical treatment for the shock he witnessed. When Jon got up and turned on the lights, all he could do was scream when he saw the bed and the blood.

I must have been quite a sight, lying there in bed, bleeding all over the place. I guess my arm and my ribs were a sight also. I was bleeding from six places on my little body, I needed medical attention and fast. From what I learned, the doctors were told I tripped and fell down the steps. However, this whole event was played back to me, time and again, by the doctors at the hospital to try and discover what had happened to me. They seemed to know a mere fall wouldn't cause the damage I'd received. The amount of blood I lost was incredible, from what I heard. I lay there in the hospital, trying to recover from the pain I'd endured. I was told a piece of skull was on my brain, about the size of my little fingernail, it had to be removed. I remained in intensive care for two weeks before they moved me to a standard care ward.

Folks, are you starting to get the picture that my brother and I weren't wanted? I'm a fast learner, and I didn't want to go through this again. It took three weeks to recover from this tragedy. When I did, the state authorities were waiting to take us to another home. I'm sure that some of you are asking what happened to our stepfather. When the authorities found out what happened, and were sure of the events and the way they played out, they went after him.

Apparently, our stepfather was a truck driver. They discovered he was on a west coast run delivering material. The events are vague, but from what I managed to put together from our new house mother, they were chasing him in the mountains of southern California, when his truck wrecked and he was killed at the scene. A fitting end to someone who would hurt an innocent child. It was fortunate he met his end that way. In the South, they don't take kindly to men who hurt children. He got off easy.

Jon and I moved on with our lives after this short and disastrous moment with our mother. From that moment on, we wouldn't see her again until she was on her deathbed in a Tennessee hospital. That chapter, and the events that transpired, will be held for later.

CHAPTER 4

Jon and I were sent to the final state home we would be placed in. If you lost count, we were placed in a total of five. I'm thankful, at least until I tell you about this one. The school we were placed in was for children who were abused, unwanted, malcontents, unlearned, and disgruntled. Get the picture? We fit all of the above, so why not? Do you think the pain and abuse stopped here? You'll find out, as you read further.

This last stop for us was a huge school with over seven hundred children, ranging from the age of three years to eighteen years, girls and boys. The girl's dorms were at one end of the campus, the boy's dorms at the other. You can guess why—to keep us apart—even I knew that score by now. This place was a little different than the others. Here we had real house mothers that tried to raise us as children were supposed to be raised. They had problems with some of the kids, and when they did, they always called the counselors assigned to each child, who would come to the dorms and take care of the problem teenagers.

Being new to this place, as with every home we were sent to, we had to be indoctrinated to the rules like everyone else. So as you might guess, we were on the blunt end of a lot of practical jokes. When in Rome, do as the Romans do, but learn quickly. Jon and I stayed to ourselves as much as possible. There was always something to learn and do, so we tried a little bit of everything as we grew. If you haven't guessed by now, my brother and I were exactly twelve years old. We were learning quickly what things worked and what didn't. We knew we weren't going to see, or live with, our parents again, so we knew we had to coexist here or die. There simply wasn't another school for the state to put us in, other than a detention ward, which wasn't exactly a cup of tea. Jon and I hadn't caused any major trouble, other than that which we gave to the ex-prison guard who hurt my brother. There was something strange about that incident, as I learned later. However, I couldn't change things; they were as they were, and our lives were to take on a new meaning here. I had to try and let the past take care of itself!

When we were assigned a counselor, he read us our case history from a folder the child services people gave him. We sat at his desk, as he read every event that might have anything to do with us causing trouble or mischief, and I mean every event. All the state had chosen to include, that is! I noticed some of the dramatic events in our story were missing, especially the bull-whipping event. Wonder why that is? Congressmen and senators from the great states in the South set up funding for all these schools. For any negative events to leak out about how children were treated and leaking to the press would have dramatic consequences. These events, no matter how bad they might seem, or as negative they might be, were conveniently swept under the rug.

This was my first lesson in politics. Kiss the babies, make no waves, and do unto others before they do unto you. The type of cordial back-slapping, as we call it in the South. As our counselor read, I discovered the beatings my brother took while at the same school were also missing, along with the incident of me almost being killed by my supposed stepfather. I found out later our uncle had given one of the counselors at the detention unit some money in order to let us visit our mother. I certainly wished that moment hadn't happened. I was learning how things were done in the South and the way politics played out. As you read about the future events that unfold, these politics will come back to haunt a lot of people. Now you realize why I'm hiding the names of a lot of people in my past. It isn't that I'm afraid of what might transpire. Hell, after all I've been through, there isn't much that scares me today except the cries of a little child. I'm still not used to that. It must be from all the crying I remember back in my childhood growing up. I don't know if I'll ever forget the memory of those cries. They haunt me to this day!

When the counselor finished reading our past from the file, the strangest thing happened. This man looked over the desk, and asked if we were going to be trouble. Exactly why he asked that, I haven't a clue. We were the ones being hurt and abused, and to ask us this question was pure horse..., oops, got to keep it clean. I sat there, looking back in my memory about all we had gone through, and I was frankly amazed he was asking this question, stupid as it was. I replied that we were here to learn and move on with our lives, and we would be on our best behavior. He replied that we had better be, and if not, we would pay the price. We were sitting here and being labeled as troublemakers; however we were the ones who almost died on numerous occasions and all the while, under state jurisdiction. You do the math. What's wrong with this picture?

I told you politics were to become very important in our lives, and we would learn quickly why the state did things as they did. My brother and I didn't exactly fit in here as well as you might think. We both had chips on our shoulders from all the pain we'd gone through, and we were quick to let people know if they disrespected us in any way there would be a price to pay. I couldn't have been more wrong. The first night as we sat in study hall, our housemother called out everyone's name, I received my first taste of getting put in my place! She got to my name and butchered the pronunciation badly. I corrected her, and guess what her response was? She asked, "What did you say?" I replied, "My name is Fulghum."

She replied, "Is that so? Come here, please." Stupid me didn't see what was coming. I got up and walked over to her, and when I got there, she arose from her chair, quick as a cat, grabbed me by the hair of the head, and slammed me against the wall. When she did this, she had my full attention. She said my name was whatever she wanted to say it was, and I would answer her as she wanted. After that one lesson in diction, we didn't have another problem for the rest of my seven years under her direction.

In this particular school, everyone on campus went to school. In other words, no busing, just get up, learn the routine every day, do what was expected of you, and you didn't get into any trouble. If you chose to disregard the program you paid. Brother, did you pay!

This school was just like any other school, except you lived at school and you went to school learning many things. We had vocational departments, which served those who wanted to learn a vocation in cosmetology, printing, auto mechanics, woodworking, metal trades, and welding. There was a lot you could learn, if you were willing, and some things you didn't want to learn about, as you will find out. I remember watching and learning from a lot of kids there, some things I wished I'd never known. We had our share of troubles, including drugs and racial equality. When it came to the state and politics, these last two were strictly taboo. You didn't talk about drugs, and you certainly didn't talk about racial problems. These wouldn't be tolerated at all. If you chose to speak your mind, they didn't mind bending your skull and correcting you!

We weren't there very long when we noticed things happening that reminded us of the first home we were sent to. Remember the crying in the night, and the panic we felt whenever someone was being taken advantage of? The same problems existed here. Jon and I were very close to each other. We always watched each other's backs, especially at night! I remember one night, a large boy came over to my bed and wanting to get in with me. Naturally, I objected. When I did, he hit me in the face. Big mistake, he never knew what hit him. Jon was awake and watching as the guy started hitting me. My brother got up out of bed, hauled off, and kicked him right in the privates. When he fell, we both were on him like cats. He was now screaming bloody murder. This caused a lot of commotion and alerted the house mother. She came in with this huge paddle and asked what was going on. When we told her what happened, she looked down at the boy holding his privates in one hand, and his bloody nose in the other. She asked him if this was true. He sat there and nodded his head yes. She took one look at him, then grabbed him by the hair of the head, and dragged him out of the room, telling everyone to get back in bed, and if she heard one peep there would be hell to pay! My brother and I were elated. We were also scared because we knew this boy had friends and we thought for sure they would come and seek some form of revenge. But it never came. That

33

night, Jon and I earned a reputation—if you messed with one of us you were getting two for the price of one. Big trouble if you didn't know any better.

Things weren't always that easy though. There were always times when we were separated, and things happened, I care not to mention or bring back to memory from the dark closets of my mind. Each of us there had our share of bad moments, because you simply couldn't beat everyone, and there were always times when there were more than one boy could whoop. Even using your imagination, you'll never touch or grasp the full magnitude of events that transpired. These are events that until this day I haven't discussed with anyone, including my wife or children. In many ways I figured it was the cross I had to bear and live with. I certainly didn't ask for it, but it was there and as with everything in life, you had to deal with it and move on. It still doesn't make life any easier to endure or live with.

One particular evening, my brother and I were separated, and these boys were up to no good. They were trying to have their way with Jon. Someone heard the commotion and alerted me where he was. I grabbed a bat and went to his aid, but I didn't arrive in time. I vowed, from that moment on, if anyone ever touched me or my brother, in any fashion, in any way, they had better kill us! I'd had enough, and I wasn't going to stand there and take it anymore.

I made this statement in study hall, where everyone had to be at a special time each evening. I said it in the face of everyone there, including our house mother, who acted like nothing was going on at all. As you might guess, you can't make threats without getting into trouble. However, after that night, you know what happened? We were only tried once after that, and the boy who tried it got a full case of broken ribs for his actions.

I received full detention after my remarks, but it was worth it. The boys attacking us stopped and went their own way. I made a stand, as I would have to on many occasions. The fights didn't get easier for any of us. Each day, we had to learn something new, sometimes the hard way. It was the way to survive. I believe we could have learned easier. I learned as I went, but it never came easy.

The greatest moments were when I could protect my brother. It seemed the beatings my brother got before we came to this school took all the fight out of him. He didn't care to fight at all, and he would give in rather than fight his way out of a situation. Not me. I didn't care. If I had to fight, so be it. Even if I lost, I wasn't going to make it easy for anyone. People soon started realizing that fact, and in many ways, it was a new awakening for us. Things didn't necessarily get any easier; however people started giving us our due. They soon started calling me the crazy Fulghum, because I would go off the deep end if they tried anything with me or my brother. I gained respect—no, I earned it. I stopped letting people push me around. Much as life will if you let it, there are always going to be people in this world that will take and take from you if you allow them to. I just learned what was perhaps the most important lesson in my young life—if you don't respect yourself others won't and will most certainly take advantage of you. I learned quick, but there were other kids that weren't as successful as we were.

They paid the price with their lives. Some couldn't take the pain and the torment, and they would take their own lives. I hope you remember this comment. I spoke of it earlier, at the first school we were sent to when we were only two years old.

Death isn't pretty. I've seen my share of kids that couldn't cope with life as we knew it, and took care of the situation the only way they knew how. I knew kids, beautiful kids, girls and boys, who were tormented by abuse, hurt, and neglect. There isn't much in life that prepares you for what we were going through. I've never read a book that informs anyone how they're to respond to the kind of torment we saw and felt each day we lived in those schools. I'm sure there will be many who will question the comments and quality of events I'm writing about. However, I'm not going anywhere and I stopped running long ago. For those people who might challenge my comments, I will always stand ready to defend my right to express my opinion. I can and will back up everything I am writing in this book.

There simply isn't enough time to list all my comments, or examples of a life that I went through along with many others. The principles that were involved are probably gone and buried, but the kids that endured and live to this day, are a living testament to the truth that exists. These few kids are my inspiration to let others know how we lived, and more importantly survived, through it all. The state might try to defend their position, and say they developed our will and made us survivors. They, my friends, are liars. They will never earn my respect for what I saw and endured those many years under their direct tutelage. Let them try. There are many of us who remain, who will always disagree.

Enough of my preaching. I need to get back to the important part of my story. In many ways, this story isn't about me or my brother. It is about the fact we were a part of a group of children who were just like us in many ways. Many of them had parents who loved them and wanted them, but there were problems that existed to prevent most of them from returning to their families. There were problems and reasons why many of the other kids never found their way back to their loving families. Some reasons are best left unsaid; however if you search deep enough, the reasons exist to this day.

Jon and I weren't fortunate enough to be among the lucky ones. We didn't have anyone who cared about us. That's what made us different from all the others. Jon and I were only visited once in the entire period we were under state's care. Sixteen years of utter and bitter loneliness. Not once did any member of our supposed family ever reach out and try to make us feel welcome. This is the bitterest of pills to swallow. The fact we survived at all is a living testament to the belief and will we had for ourselves. I believe with all my heart we were created for a divine purpose in life. I read that, or heard it somewhere long ago. There's one thing I'm convinced of. Our dear Heavenly Father gave us a mind to think and explore our horizons and to make our own decisions in life! I chose to use my life for the better and chose the exact opposite of how I was raised. All of my experiences have prepared me for the life I now live. On with our story.

The hardest thing I've discovered about being raised the way we were was the constant struggle to distinguish right from wrong, but not in the sense of morally right or wrong. It was the responsible sense I'm referring to. Everywhere I looked, each day, there were choices to be made, important ones that could change or alter the complete structure of my future if I chose incorrectly. I will explain, however let me present you with a little foretaste. My brother and I lived our lives without a mothering touch. What exactly does that mean? It's very simple. We were never held as children, loved, cradled, read to, sung to, or nurtured in a loving environment. We only had each other to live with. It amazes me to this day how we survived at all. I read somewhere once that case studies were performed in the 1950s and '60s, where there were children—babies to be exact—taken and placed in total solitude, to see how they would react. Some of the babies reverted to nothing more than a shell, and others died. I struggled with this, because I was raised in an environment that didn't allow my brother and I to feel these simple and endearing factors. We missed out on some of the most precious moments in life that countless others take for granted. Now don't get me wrong, we did receive praise and forms of love from time to time, from doing our chores or performing well in school. However, these aren't the same types of praises!

Our lives were forever changed by the way we were raised. The simplest form of pleasure we knew was being together and nurturing each other. How, you ask? Imagine yourself out on an island. There isn't anyone else around, and all you have for company is your brother. This is how we felt. There were others around us, of course. But no one cared deeply if we lived or died—no one except ourselves. We would revel in the fact when we discovered something positive, and in these few and precious moments we grew a little. This wasn't always the case. There were times when we would go off by ourselves, just sit and hold each other and try to understand why we were alone. Folks, this is wrong. No child should have to endure this type of life. We did, though, and we made the best of it. We were always alone, but we knew we had each other for comfort and support. This was all we needed.

In my short and meager life, I'd only trusted one person—my brother, and he in me. It was all we had. Believe me, when I say we tried to let others in our world, we did! But we found out in time there were ulterior motives to their friendship. Some had too high a price, so we reverted to our little world and grew as best as we knew how. I've always said I have acquaintances in life, but very few friends. This is the case today. I can honestly say, the only friend I had in life up to this point was my brother, and I'm sure he would say the same of me! As difficult as it is to say, it was true. I've discovered true friends will always try to guide and protect you from harm. They will give of themselves without asking for anything in return. I discovered this simple truth the hard way, time and time again. It always formed my basis for the truest of friendships and remains the constant variable for friends in my life today. I learned to watch and value what others do around me, decide if they fit into my world, and more importantly into my brother's world. I was responsible for him and he for me. We were all we had, and until later it was all we could trust and believe in.

This school was just like the others we were raised in, except this one was huge. The entire campus covered almost six hundred acres, and for Jon and I, this was one huge, magical world. We had a large farm with cattle, goats, chickens, pigs, and produce growing everywhere. I thought everything grown on our farm was there for the needs of the children. I will explain later just how wrong I was.

We discovered everyday conditions were exactly like all the other schools we were placed in. There was visitation day every second weekend of every month, and the children who had parents or family were allowed to have visitors on campus out in the open for Saturday and Sunday, four hours each day. For many of the children, these were the happiest days of the week, but for others who were in the same boat as my brother and I, it was a miserable period. My brother and I didn't dwell on it and always went to the ball field to play games and try not to notice how things transpired between the other kids and their families. It was hard, but we knew the score. It was something we were accustomed to. It was also something we couldn't do anything about, so we went off by ourselves to try and discover our new world and make the most of our lives.

There were times, however, when we couldn't help but notice these visitation periods. We watched the other kids and imagined what joy they must have felt and how happy they must have been, if only for that short period. It didn't take a rocket scientist to realize something was wrong with this picture, but some things never changed no matter how wrong they were. Imagine a life with no birthdays, Christmases, or special holidays to celebrate, if you could, and you would see Jon and me, by ourselves with each other, trying to cope and make the best of things. Don't get me wrong, it sounds like we felt sorry for ourselves. We didn't. We had been through this countless times before. It wasn't something new for us, but it doesn't mean we weren't hurt or lonely. We were. We just didn't let it show to others around us!

Now for folks out there reading this and getting misty eyed, you should understand this wasn't entirely bad. Why? If you've never had special moments in your life that you enjoy, you never miss out on them, correct? The only times my brother and I experienced pain was when the other children made a big deal of things. They would show off their new clothes, shoes, toys, and other things they received. It would then hit home what we were missing. But listen, and believe what I'm about to say—my brother and I couldn't have cared less about material things or the gifts the other children received. We cared about more important things. Those were the moments when we would see children receiving hugs and kisses, tender acts of love, and expressions of enlightenment on the faces of children we saw that were moved by the enjoyment of simply being with someone who cared. This is what Jon and I wanted the most. It was what we lived for!

In my entire childhood, I can tell you honestly, I would have killed for the love of an adult or a parent that would hold me and tell me they loved me. I simply can't remember ever being told I was special or have someone say to me those few endearing words we so longed to hear—"I love you." These were words that meant the most to us, and I can't remember them being said to me by anyone other than my brother. It always amazed me when I saw other children being disrespectful to their parents; I thought to myself—were it me in their place, it would be much different. The sight of such an act turned my stomach as much as anything. If any other child had been placed in our world for a month, they would change their act real quick. I was amazed when a new kid would come to our school. They would act tough and strong-willed for awhile; however you could see a difference in them in the space of a few weeks. They changed, sometimes for the good, sometimes not. You could never tell with some kids exactly how long it would take; however one thing was certain—they would change, even the toughest. It was only a matter of time.

Jon and I moved on with our lives and tried to set ourselves up to perform the best we could in everything. We weren't happy with just succeeding. We had to be the best in everything we did, and we set high standards for ourselves. We didn't always succeed however we weren't lost for our efforts.

There were always things to do at this school. The state made sure that you did your share of work. Remember the farm and livestock I spoke about earlier? Guess who took care of it and fed and cleaned up after those animals? That's right, all of the children on campus were assigned regular duties after they were indoctrinated into the school program. The first job we were given was laundry detail. Now hang on to your hats, ladies and gentleman, and imagine this if you will—there were exactly eight dorms on campus for the boys and seven dorms for the girls. Every child had a bed of their own, and each bed had two sheets that required washing twice a week, and please don't get me started on all the clothes for everyone. Think of this, with sixty-five children in a dorm, fifteen dorms on campus, and two sheets to every bed. That is a hell of a lot of sheets. For the next six months, three to four hours each day after school, we had to go to the laundry building, and clean, dry, and fold all the laundry for the entire campus. We weren't the only ones assigned to do this. There were a total of one hundred and twenty-eight children assigned to this detail, and it worked like clockwork. You had to do this particular detail in order to move on and graduate to the next level of the work detail.

Folks, after you read this section, please show it to your children and let them try to understand just exactly how great they have things at home. The next time they complain about something, stick them into the laundry detail in your home and see if they like it. I believe you will find their attitude will change. If not, let them read the rest of the work details I'm going to explain. They'll change for sure!

I did the math once; the total number of sheets we had to do every week was a whopping 3900 sheets and pillow cases, each and every week for six months. Now try asking junior to wash his jeans the next time he gets them dirty. Believe me, he will change. If not, he's stupid! Our laundry building had six industrial washing machines that could wash about four hundred sheets in each load. We also had four steam presses where we would take the sheets from end to end on one side, feed them into the press, and the sheet would be fed through huge rollers that would press and dry each sheet in about thirty seconds. Then we would have to fold each sheet nice and neat, and stack them into baskets to be delivered to the dorms for each bed change out. It didn't take us long to get tired of doing laundry; however it did make the time go by. After we finished our time doing laundry detail, we were sent to the cafeteria to eat dinner each evening. After working as hard as we did each day, we were hungry, and would eat anything, although there were times when we would go through the dinner line and sometimes we couldn't stomach what we saw. We'd turn around, go back to the dorm, and do without. We didn't do this very often, as we learned to appreciate, and even stomach, what was served.

We did our duties each day, seven days a week, and accepted this as life. Just another hint at something junior or missy might not understand. We weren't given a dime, not one red cent! Think about that the next time your children need extra spending money. In fact, let them know all the work details we were assigned to over the space of seven years and were never paid one dime. Gives new meaning to slave labor, doesn't it?

Jon and I made the most of everything we had, but we did learn ways to earn extra money from other kids on campus, if they didn't want to do their work detail. We would work for them but they had to pay up front first—a lesson I learned the hard way! Jon and I would do three to four extra details each week, and earned one to two dollars each time we did someone else's chores, depending on the detail and the person we worked for! Each time we finished, Jon and I would rush off to the store up the street from campus, about a mile away. We would buy some candy or a soda, anything we could afford. We would then go and sit down under a tree, and share with each other whatever we had bought from the store. This act was special and very important for both of us. I couldn't, and wouldn't ever eat or drink anything without my brother there to get his share. This, for you stingy little brats out there in fantasyland, is sharing and giving to its fullest.

Every day was a learning experience and we accepted every challenge with open arms. Let me explain why. When you are constantly challenged, in a world where rules are made to be obeyed, you find special interest in exploring ways to challenge those rules and beat them. This was of particular interest to my brother and I, because the state had too many rules. We saw fit to break as many of those rules as we could get away with. Just what type of rules, and how did we go about breaking them? Jon and I were identical twins. The only thing you could see on our face that was different was a little mole that I have on the left side of my face. When we went to school, we always tried to dress alike. We discovered it would drive our teachers crazy trying to figure out who was who.

My strong suit in school was math, and my brother's was history. Guess what our weak subjects were, for the both of us? We were both weak where the other was strong. So being ingenious and bright children—so we thought—we decided to see if we could get away with our idea and try to fool our teachers. We did for

39

a while. Whenever we had a class and knew there was going to be a test given, we would switch with each other. We would ace the test every time, but as all good plans go, we got caught.

I haven't the foggiest idea how the teachers found out, but they did, and boy, talk about getting upset and downright pissed! The principal called us into his office one day, and guess who was standing there with him in his office? Our history and math teacher. Do you want to know what they asked us to do? They made us each take the exams for that day again, and guess what happened? I failed the history exam, and Jon failed the math exam. When we were given the next test, I passed the math test and Jon passed the history exam. Upon seeing the results, you can imagine when the principal got through with us, our bottoms hurt, and we had to repeat the last semester over during the summer session while everyone else was enjoying the summer. Did we learn anything? Yes, we did. We didn't switch class as much anymore after that, but in time we knew it wasn't doing either of us any good, so we started helping each other out instead. We worked hard and put forth an honest effort, trying to achieve the best grade we could. After we started going to our own classes, it was always worth a good laugh to see the teachers trying to figure out if we were still switching class. They never caught us after that time, though it didn't matter. We still got a huge laugh out of it!

I remember an old saying that, "Good things happen to good people." However, there is another saying, "Bad things also happen to bad people." Remember that kid named Joe, who hurt me on the mountain? You'll never guess who showed up one day at this school.

Jon and I were sitting out on the steps of the high school one day, and we observed a counselor walking through the door with five new students. One of the boys was that snake in the grass, good for nothing, Joe. He walked right by me. He didn't recognize me or even take a second look! I was afraid that he might, but when he didn't, I thanked my lucky stars and rushed off the porch and back to our dorm, with my brother hot in pursuit. When I got to my locker, I explained to my brother exactly why I was so excited.

I told him about the incident on the mountain, and exactly what happened to me in Joe's room. He got mad as hell, and if you think Jon was mad, I was madder. I told him what I wanted to do to this boy, and I had waited a long time for payback. If I had the heart to share with you exactly what this boy did to me, this book would be X-rated and too obscene for children to read. That's why I won't explain in detail, so use your imagination and you might perceive to have a small glimpse of what I went through. The boy even laughed at me when I ran from his room. It was payback time. All I had to do was wait until I found the right moment and strike.

I'm sure there are some of you reading this and saying to yourselves that violence isn't the answer, and you're correct. But this boy bragged to his friends about what he did to me. I had to endure pain and guilt for an awful long time, at least for as long as I was on that mountain. And now it was my time to return some of the pain I had suffered. I wasn't about to be denied! My brother and I watched, waited, and guess what happened? Good things do happen to good people, and those good people were Jon and myself. There was an empty bed in our dorm and guess who got assigned the bed? Joe was assigned to the bed across the lockers from us and I was elated. He walked by us again and still didn't recognize me. so I knew then all I had to do was wait for the right moment and give him his due!

I'm not a vindictive person, and I don't go around planning events that will intentionally hurt someone, but this was different. I had to let this boy know I hadn't forgotten what he did to me, and I was going to make sure he didn't forget me either. Now, I had one honest thought as I was trying to work things out. I have no idea how many kids this boy attacked at the other schools, like he did me. I know that with me he had gotten away with it—or so he thought. I honestly took it upon myself to make sure that he didn't plan or do anything to ever hurt anyone again, especially while he was here at this school.

I'm sure everyone is trying to figure out exactly what my plan might be. I waited until one day when I knew everyone would be outside. That was visitation day. All the boys in the dorm were out playing. I had my brother go and ask Joe if he wanted to play a game, and to my utter surprise and amazement, he said yes. Why, I don't know, but he did, and without knowing any better, he walked right into my trap.

We played a game of cards called rummy for cookies. Joe played along and he was doing all right. If anyone came by and looked at us, you would swear we were having a pretty good time. I started asking Joe about some of the homes he had been placed in. He told us about a few; however he didn't mention the school on the mountain. I wondered if I was mistaken. Could this be the wrong boy? When he didn't take the bait and give the answer I was wanting to hear, I did it for him. I asked him directly, never taking my eyes off his for one moment, about a school on a mountain. He answered yes, he had been there for seven years, and to my utter delight he asked me if I had been there as well. I did and I told him my name. Have you ever watched a scary movie when the victim discovers they're about to become the next one to fall into harm's way? This is exactly what happen to Joe. His mouth opened, and he started to get up. He never made it. All the time I was talking to him, my brother had gotten up off the bed and was standing directly behind Joe. He was waiting for my signal. When I gave it, I simply dropped the cards from my hands, and my brother grabbed him before he could do anything.

Now Joe was a big kid, some thirty or forty pounds heavier than we were; however when there are two of you, it evens the odds. My brother and I pushed him down on the bed. I looked at him and told him I had waited a long time to finally pay him back for the humiliation he caused me so long ago on that mountain. Now it was payback time. Would you like to know what happened next? Joe started pleading and begging, much as I had when he held me down and hurt me, but today my ears were deaf. Begging wasn't going to work! For the sake of those readers, young and old, I'm not going to disclose exactly what I did to Joe, but it was just and swift. I didn't do to him what he did to me. I couldn't and wouldn't.

41

That wasn't my style, but he got my message loud and clear. I will tell you this though—there would be lots of pain in his life after that moment upstairs with my brother and I. He would always remember who and what caused him that pain, I'm certain of that!

There was one thing I was certain of—Joe's days of hurting others would soon be behind him! When we let him go he ran from us, much as I had years before; however I didn't laugh. What I did wasn't funny, and it wasn't meant to be. It was a lesson taught from sheer hatred! You know what the best part was? Joe ran away from school the very next night. We never saw him again. I believe it was convenient for him in many ways! It was his word against ours, if he told anyone. I believe he thought long and hard about some of the harm he had caused others in his life and figured he got off easy!

I wasn't exactly pleased with myself after that day. I had carried a heavy cross for so long. To finally seek my revenge didn't make me feel any better about myself. I still bore the memory of what happened to me, and it wasn't pleasant. I felt empty, but it did change me. I didn't hurt anyone else like I did Joe, ever again. I also learned revenge isn't as sweet as some might think. I did have a conscience. I didn't like myself for awhile; however I learned what was important and I moved on. That part of my life was like water running under a bridge. It ran past me and was long gone. I couldn't bring it back.

I was to remember that time for a while. Jon and I carried on with our lives as if nothing had happened. Joe's counselor did come and ask us some questions about what we had seen and heard; however we'd been through this drill before. We knew the drill and what to do and say. Before long, Joe's memory vanished, just like water passing under the bridge of life, gone and forgotten.

CHAPTER 5

My brother and I went on with our lives. We soon found ourselves back in the mainstream of life, at least as we knew it. We went back out to daily duties and discovered we weren't any different from the other children who surrounded us, we were simply the ones who didn't have anyone. But we did have something special in our lives that perhaps made us different from the other children—desire, sheer, unquestionable desire, to become more than we were ever meant to be.

You're probably thinking we had structure presented to us by the state and were given examples of what we could become if we followed their lead. Wrong. If my brother and I had followed the direction the state showed us, I sincerely believe both of us would either be dead or in prison today. I was given a choice when I was very little. That choice was either to give up and follow, or take the world by the horns and walk the road of life by myself. I think you know by now which road I chose. How in the world could I follow those whom I couldn't trust and didn't give two cents if we succeeded or failed? So I chose my own path, and difficult as it was, I'm happy with the results. I'm alive today, which is more than I can say for many of the unfortunate children we lived with, who came and went frequently from these same schools.

Jon and I were different, we didn't have anyone whom we trusted to discuss our problems with. Having no one in whom we could trust presented us with many difficult situations, as you might guess. When these difficult situations came up, Jon and I would go off by ourselves to discuss what the problems were and try to rationalize the situation, as well as two little boys could. We would try to discover the best solution for what we had to do and how we thought it best to resolve the situation. Now, for many of you laypeople out there who are thinking this is a bunch of crap, think again. My brother and I didn't trust anyone in life. The few times we had, we found ourselves hurt more than we were helped. For two little boys, this was bewildering.

Jon and I had a special gift for choosing and discussing each situation out and exploring our options in just about every problem that arose. We would go off by ourselves and sit and talk. There were many times, if the situation was difficult, we would draw close and simply hold each other. We found out very early in life that this simple gesture made each of us feel comfortable and helped us discuss our problems. For some of you who might not understand what was happening here, let me explain. If there isn't anyone else in life around to hold you when things are tough, and you feel all alone and need a hug, whom do you go to when there's no one around?

From as far back as I could remember, we were the only ones to give each other hugs. When you only have each other, you develop the sincerest of trust. For the other kids around us, this seemed strange. We were constantly called bitter names that I detest with every moral fiber of my being. This was our little world. To have anyone challenge something that was sacred and pure to us was the lowest act of indecency. After a while our skin got tough and we didn't care what others thought. All that mattered to us was we were together. If I needed a hug, or someone to hold my hand, I always went to my brother, and he to me.

In time this came to be accepted by those around us; however there were always weird looks from time to time. We accepted them, moved on, and closed others off from our lives. This was a gift, something that helped us tremendously. Neither one of us really cared what others thought. They weren't who were important to us. What we considered important was we had one person we could depend on. When things got tough we always had something wonderful we could fall back on, and more importantly, depend on explicitly.

Jon and I were constantly depending on each other. Things always seemed to work out one way or another. Sometimes for good, other times for bad. I never said we were perfect, but we were getting better every day in our decision-making process.

We continued on in our duties around school with each season and birthdays that came. You might think birthdays were something special for us. Wrong. It was just another day to us; no one made anything special of it, no one ran up the flag or celebrated this event, so we took it in stride and moved on. This wasn't always the case though. We couldn't help but notice when other kids around us did celebrate their birthday, Christmas, or other special holidays.

We were human and we could tell there was something going on. However, when in Rome do as the Romans do; shrug it off and move on with life. We couldn't afford getting melancholy or sympathetic over things we had no control over. It wasn't in our nature, and especially not in the makeup of things as we saw them. We could have gone off and felt sorry for ourselves, but it would have taken away from the truth of the situation, and this was always in the forefront of our minds. If it was meant for us to have something to celebrate, it would have to be something special indeed. However, the one special thing we were looking for never came, so we didn't celebrate. We were still holding out and believing one day our mother or father might show up to take us away from our situation. We looked for this one moment to come from the time we were five, until we graduated from high school. You might think we had false hopes; however everyone has to believe in something. This was our belief, as farfetched as it was. We held to it, and we never lost sight of the prize.

Jon and I were in the laundry building one day, doing our regular duties. It was summer time, with the steam presses going. It was hot and we were getting sweaty, so the lady who ran the laundry—let's call her Patty—let us take off our shirts. This was taboo, especially working around steam and other hot objects in the laundry building; however my brother and I were developing a relationship with Patty. She trusted us. It was hot on this day, and both of us were pulling a double because some of the other boys didn't want to work in the heat, especially in the summer time. They paid us and we worked their detail. We didn't tell them, but with the relationship we were building with Patty, we would have worked it for free. But we had our morals; we couldn't let them get off for nothing!

This relationship we had with Patty was unusual to say the least. For the first time I could remember, we actually were developing some trust with this lady, in some ways developing a friendship. Not a close friendship, but a friendship nonetheless. We were working hard. We always worked hard for Patty, and when we did, she gave us treats. This was something we came to like very much. When you worked hard for Patty, she always seemed to appreciate it and let you know. This hot summer day, things were going smooth, and Patty let us take off our shirts because we were sweating our tails off in that hot building. I felt like I was burning up. I didn't realize it at the time, but I was getting sick. I was developing a huge rash over the upper portion of my body, any way I didn't let it bother me and kept working hard.

Patty came over to us to stop us from what we were doing. She asked me to come over to the laundry room door and stand in the light for her, so she could take a look at me. I went over to her by the door in the sunlight. She took me by the shoulder and turned me around. She examined me and told me I had a rash over most of my back and chest and she thought I was burning up. At first, she thought I might be having an allergic reaction to the bleach and detergent we used in cleaning the laundry. We used some potent industrial soap powder and bleach products, and there were times kids got an allergic reaction to them. She thought it best to send me back to the dorm and rest for a while and come back later if I felt like it. I argued as best I could, because I enjoyed what we were doing and I enjoyed Patty's company even more. She was one of the few adults who were kind to my brother and I. However, she insisted, so I went to the dorm to lay down and relax.

I don't have any idea how long I slept but I was awakened by my brother, who told me I had missed dinner and that I was burning up. Jon went to our house mother and told her he thought I was ill and asked if she could check on me. This is where things get really strange. From early on in our childhood my brother and I learned, you don't ask a house mother to stop what they're doing and come and check on someone. They didn't like to be disturbed. They have a life and a family, and they tried to live as normal a life as possible without having to be interrupted.

The house mother came as asked, and was, shall we say, a little ticked she'd been interrupted. When she got to my bedside, she found me hot, flushed, and sweating profusely. She was a little alarmed; however she was in the middle of a show she was watching on television, and she wanted to get back to it. She simply told my brother and I to go to the infirmary. I could hardly stand up without falling down. I needed my brother's help to guide me down the hall and down the two flights of steps out the building, because when I stood up, the room started spinning, I got dizzy, and I couldn't manage on my own. This took place with the house mother standing there, and not saying a word.

Today with my children, if they are sick and I saw they needed medical attention, I never, and I repeat never, would send them on their own. I'd carry them if the need exists! I was burning up with a fever. No one can perform or walk correctly, let alone cross a street, under this type of circumstance. My brother had to almost carry me. I was only thirteen years old at the time and weighed about one hundred pounds. My brother was about the same. We were normal kids, and he couldn't carry me, even if he wanted to. Jon managed as well as he could, and I could tell by the look in his eyes that he was concerned. I was so delirious I had no idea how long it took us to get there. When we arrived, Jon sat me down on the bench in the lobby and ran to get the nurse. I was sick, real sick. I didn't have any idea how sick I was; however I sat there rocking back and forth, awaiting the nurse to come examine me. My brother finally found her and asked her to come and help me. She calmly walked down the hall to look at me. When the nurse arrived, she immediately asked me what I'd been into. Now folks, I hardly knew where I was, let alone how to answer that question. My brother tried to explain, but the nurse stopped him and told him abruptly, she was talking to me! I passed out completely and fell to the floor. The nurse thought I was faking, as some kids would do to get out of class, and she nudged me with her foot, as my brother told me later. She reached down to grab my arm, and said, "Come on, you little faker." When she did, she felt the heat from my arm. Jon said her face went pale and she got scared. Jon would tell me later that she screamed and called for help, and an office attendant came running to help her. When he arrived, he took one look at me and said, "Oh my God!"

He told the nurse she'd better call the doctor and get him here quick! She did as he instructed and called the doctor. The attendant picked me up and took me to a bed, where he got me undressed. The nurse came back and said the doctor was on his way and would be there in about an hour. She took my temperature and found it was a little over one hundred and four. She called the doctor's office and explained my condition. He told her to pack me in ice, and he would be there shortly.

What they did saved my life. I had come down with scarlet fever. Back in those days this was contagious and very dangerous. The only good thing that came from this whole episode was my brother was there, and they let him stay with me until the doctor arrived.

When the doctor came in to examine me, he told everyone to clear the room and told the nurse that absolutely no one was to be allowed in the room except him and hospital staff. I say "hospital," because the medical staff there always spoke of this place as our little hospital, and not an infirmary, like the house mothers called it. The doctor told the nurse she was to wear scrubs and a mask, because adults could catch scarlet fever as well as children, and it was dangerous! The doctor told the nurse she was to advise the house mother in charge to look at all the kids and send anyone over if they felt like they had a fever. Strange, don't you think, that the doctor wouldn't examine them himself? I always wondered about that! However, he also instructed the nurse to make sure I had plenty of water to drink, because the way I was sweating, and with the cold shakes to come, if I weren't properly hydrated, I could go into convulsions or what he called cardiac arrest. Do you get the idea I should have been sent to a real hospital and taken care of there? At our infirmary there were only three nurses on staff, one for each eight-hour period. Taking care of me properly was going to involve a lot of attention, and our nurses weren't exactly efficient at taking care of someone in my condition. I had another problem with this as well. This fever, contagious as it was, could affect even the hospital staff. Nurse T., as I will call her, was scared to death. She had never contracted the disease before, and she wasn't about to now! She had a real problem with this, and after the doctor had written his orders in my file, she hardly ever came in to check on me.

I was in the hospital for about three days, and I got very thirsty. I was sweating like a race horse running the Kentucky Derby. I needed fluids bad, and I called as best I could for the nurse, but she never came. I even went as far as knocking my metal bowl off the table, making all kinds of racket, but she never came. I only knew of one place left to get water, so I crawled out of bed and toward my bathroom, where I could see the toilet. That's right, I said my toilet. In my current condition, I couldn't stand up or walk, so I crawled. I couldn't reach the sink, so the only resource left to me was the toilet.

All of you out there reading this are probably thinking to yourself that if you were there, and this were your child, this wouldn't be happening. Correct, but you weren't there and this wasn't your child.

This is just one of the everyday misfortunes kids under the state's direction have to live with. I was almost there, I could see the water in the bowl, when to my surprise, the doctor walked through the door and asked me what I thought I was doing. I explained, as best I could, that I was thirsty and getting a drink. When any doctor gives an order they expect it to be followed, and followed to the tee, or there is going to be hell to pay!

The doctor reached down, picked me up, and carried me back to bed. After he covered me up, he went to the door, and I will never forget him yelling at the top of his lungs, as long and loud as he could, for Nurse T. When she got there and didn't enter the room, the doctor asked her when was the last time she had checked on me. She replied that it was an hour ago. He turned to me and asked if I remembered her coming in to check on me. I told him I hadn't seen her all day. To keep things in perspective, I never saw Nurse T. after that day. I really don't know what happened to her, all I know is after that day, I had all the fluids I wanted from that moment on. Someone always checked on me every hour. I found out later from the scuttlebutt around campus that Nurse T. explained to the doctor that she was scared; she had never caught scarlet fever before and was afraid to catch it. That didn't justify her neglecting a patient, and she was fired. I was in the infirmary for over two and a half weeks, until they were sure I had recovered. After a total exam, the doctor released me and said I could go back to my dorm.

I went into the hospital weighing about one hundred pounds. When I was released, I only weighed eighty-five. I was as pale as a ghost. I remember this because of two distinct things—first, I arrived at the hospital in my blue jeans wearing no belt. When I left the infirmary, if I didn't hold my pants up, they fell down. I also tried to run to the dining hall, because the day they released me it was about five in the afternoon on Thursday, when chili was served. It was my favorite food at the time, and I didn't want to miss out on it. Second, all I was fed at the infirmary was potato soup. I was sick of that, and I needed solid food. I tried to run, however I could only manage a few strides at a time, then I would have to stop and walk.

It seemed like forever, but I did reach the dining hall. The distance from the dining hall to the infirmary was a little over six hundred yards, and it took me every bit of ten minutes to get there. I told you I thought I was as pale as a ghost, didn't I? When I walked into the dining hall, everyone looked up as I came through the door. They stopped talking. I guess I was quite a sight. My brother jumped up and ran to me to give me the biggest love and hug. He said I looked like crap! Jon led me over to his tray, sat me down, and went to ask the house mother if he could get me a tray of food. It was forbidden to get two trays of food, and in my present condition I don't think I could have carried it anyway. She said he could and he went to prepare me a tray. I ate everything he gave me, and when I was finished, we walked out of the hall and back to the dorm. I explained every-thing I had heard and gone through, and Jon did the same. Jon was always my informer, and I was his. After all I'd been through, I needed to be informed on all of the events of the last two weeks.

There were some instrumental events that took place after I got ill. One change the school made was, whenever a student got sick and couldn't walk or manage without assistance, the house mother in charge was to call our counselor. They in turn were to come to our dormitory, pick us up, and take us to either the hospital or the infirmary, whichever they deemed the most prudent. Second, reports covering how and why we got sick were filled out for the state's protec-tion, just in case anything serious happened. This would be used more often in the future than you could ever realize. You might say that my getting sick was a good thing. It was for the kids, but sometimes even when you have rules and reg-ulations, they're not always followed. There are always ways to bend and even break the most stringent rules and guidelines.

Just why did I tell you about this event in my life? I wanted to let you in on some of the everyday examples that kids, including my brother and I, went through each and every day we were under the state's care and guidance. I can't say this is an example of how every state school was run; however it happened to Jon and I, and many other kids I knew from the schools we were assigned to. In some ways, we thought it was normal, because it was the only way of life we knew. However, we found out differently as we grew older. It made me mad as hell when I found out the difference between family life and state life.

I couldn't do anything at that time, but perhaps this book might have a significant impact with future schools and with rules and the way they are enforced. I can only try to open people's eyes as much as they are willing to see. I also came to realize that children couldn't and wouldn't be allowed to ever have power to change policy or have a voice in saying how they're to be punished and how they're to be raised. This is what becomes of your children when they're placed in the direct care of an organization presented with the responsibility in raising the children of others. Sometimes things happen that aren't in the best interest of children; however in all fairness to the state, they did have personnel who cared and tried to change the system. However, I came to realize that their voices were a minority. If someone made too many waves they would soon sink or be placed in a position where they would quit out of frustration, unwilling to be held responsible for future events they knew would take place, simply because the system allowed them to happen. To make things clear, remember the three monkeys sitting side by side, one with his hands over his ears, the other one with his hands over his mouth, and the other over his eyes? "Hear no evil, speak no evil, and see no evil." This was how things were. If you deterred from the rule, believe me, the ship went into stormy seas and someone paid. Many times it was the children.

CHAPTER 6

Life for me and my brother resumed as quickly as it could. We soon forgot the events of my illness and moved forward. We went back to our duties and assumed things would be all right. Patty, the laundry room supervisor, was glad to see me back. She gave me a big hug when she saw me and said she'd been worried. She missed my smiling face more than anything. I've just given everyone a clue as to how my brother and I lived our lives every day we were together. I've never been one to dwell on negatives or let them control my day. My brother and I had a reputation for always smiling and being happy. Why? Because it's more presentable to others than walking around with a frown on your face making everyone else miserable. I've always been good-natured, even when I was upset. It made my day easier, and life simply had to go forward, so why not try to be as positive as possible, even in the face of adversity?

It was enough for me to see Patty again, for my brother and me to be happy, and to have things back to normal. We were always working it seemed. I didn't mind, because it took away from the boredom, especially when Patty would come around every so often and check on me to make sure I was okay and feeling back to normal. It felt good. I thought Patty's concern was heartfelt, genuine, and sincere. This was a first for Jon and I. It seemed Patty had taken a special interest in us. She wanted to know more about us, where we came from, where we were raised, and about our parents. It was hard to talk about at times, but we tried to explain when she asked us questions, and to tell her honestly about our lives. She never pried, and she seemed perplexed that we didn't have anybody, as far as family, in our lives. If she felt sorry for us, she never showed it. If she had, I wouldn't have liked it one bit. I didn't like pity. It made me feel different, something I couldn't explain at the time, but I didn't like it, and if I suspected someone was feeling sorry for us, I would clam up, shut the door, and move on. It was the way my brother and I handled things. I guess you could call it pride. We didn't have much, but pride in ourselves was all we had. If someone attacked that, we would close the door on them. However, I never felt that way with Patty. She would ask one or more questions at a time, seemingly feeling us out, without trying to pry too much. We would answer her questions, and then move on with our duties, never suspecting the events that were to transpire.

It seemed Patty was barren and couldn't have children. She and her husband, who taught at the school, tried for many years, but nothing ever happened for them. She never made any bones about it or complained, but you could always see she was sentimental about children. I guess that's why she worked at the laundry with the kids. I never heard anyone say anything bad about her. If I did, believe me, I would have set them straight.

It seemed Patty had taken a special interest in Jon and I. She took the subject home to her husband on numerous occasions, as I came to learn. She told her husband, who I will call B.M., that she had found two kids she liked. They were hard workers and proud. B.M. liked what he heard and came to check on us. We didn't realize this, but he was checking us out. From time to time he would come and eat lunch with Patty. There Jon and I would be working our tails off like happy little beavers. He would watch and check out our demeanor. My brother and I, even if we'd had a clue, couldn't have cared less. We were happy just being together, and nothing took away from that. Perhaps this is why B.M. liked us too. One day we were getting ready for dinner, standing in line to go to the dining hall, when B.M. and Patty came and asked our house mother if we could join them for dinner at their place. At first our house mother wasn't too keen about the idea, but B.M. convinced her it was in her best interest that she did as he asked. I didn't know why, nor did I care, but she relented.

Now, for everyone who's wondering how we might react to this experience, this was a first for my brother and I, as we were asked by our house mother to go with B.M. All the other kids started whistling and jeering at us. It was the kids' way of making you think you were being given special privileges. We didn't have a clue. We went and followed B.M. and Patty to their truck. B.M. and Patty's home was off campus. This was the first time in our lives, other than the time with the elderly couple, that we spent time with someone at their home. We had no idea what home was like. We never had one, saw one, or been welcome in one before, so this was going to be a treat. We had no idea what was about to transpire. B.M. was a cowboy. He and Patty had a little farm off campus, about thirty miles from the school, where he had one hundred or so acres. It was the most incredible place I'd ever seen in my life. He had six horses and it was beautiful, to say the least. My brother and I didn't think it was practical for anyone to own a horse. Anyway, we were there, walking around, and viewing this incredible place. Patty excused herself and told B.M. she needed to prepare dinner. B.M. said he needed to feed the horses and asked if we would like to help. Imagine that. We were used to being *told*, so what do you think our answer was? We jumped at the chance! Back at school, the closest we came to seeing real live horses were the two mules that pulled the produce wagon around on the farm line.

51

This was incredible. It made our hearts jump for joy. B.M. led us to the barn, and in we walked. It was huge, with eight stalls inside. B.M. exited through a huge door and started calling his horses to come to the barn! We couldn't believe our eyes. B.M. started whistling and calling, and these horses came. I'll remember the look on my brother's face as long as I live, and he will probably remember mine. Our jaws dropped, and we looked at each other in utter amazement. Those horses came right up to him and each one seemed to know which stall was their own. They walked right by us and into their stall without a fuss. We were totally amazed. "You going to help or just stare?" B.M. asked us. He told us to go up, fasten the ropes in front of each stall, and grab a bucket. We did as he said and grabbed the buckets. B.M. then filled each bucket about halfway with oats and explained to us why he fed the horses oats, what they ate, and so on. Jon and I, in all of our amazement, started firing questions at B.M. as fast as we could. He seemed delighted. It seemed he just kept explaining things to us as we asked. It seemed perfectly natural, and it seemed to make B.M. happy. He tried to explain everything we asked in laymen terms so we could understand. He told us that feeding these horses oats was good for them, it made them regular and would help their digestive tract. For us to be there, seeing this, was incredible. We watched, and before we could say anything, B.M. told us feeding the horses had a strange effect on them. We watched in sheer and utter amazement, as each and every horse relieved themselves in their stall. B.M. then prompted us to clean the mess up. You might think we would get disgusted. Nope, not us. We'd done worse. This, my friends, was nothing. Try cleaning up the bathrooms for a week, after eighteen boys in a dormitory wing. If you can do that for punishment for two weeks, this was nothing. I thought to myself that horses were cleaner than boys anyway.

It took us about an hour, removing all the hay in each stall, and putting fresh hay down. Then B.M. asked if we wanted to brush the horses. We were delighted to have this surprise asked of us. To us it was a privilege, and we were ecstatic. Jon and I spent about ten minutes on each horse, and before you knew it, we were done. B.M. said we better go in and clean up, dinner should be ready. He led us to his house. When we entered his home, it smelled like a real home was supposed to. The smell of fried chicken filled the air, with fresh cornbread, corn, and potatoes with fresh homemade gravy. I thought I'd died and gone to heaven. We washed up and went into the dining room, where B.M. and Patty were sitting there waiting for us.

I still get misty-eyed when I think back about this moment. These two wonderful people invited us into their lives and were as happy to have us there as we were to be there. It was a special moment and the room was filled with smiles. Patty showed us to our seats, we said grace, and then we feasted. Another strange thing happened there. Did you catch it? We said grace. It was the first time we'd done that, and it wouldn't be our last. B.M. picked up the chicken, took a piece, and passed the plate around and told us to eat up. He told Patty that we had earned it; he was proud of the way we'd worked for him in the barn. I remember looking at my brother and he at me. We grinned. It was a treat for us just to be where we were. It was bliss—sheer, unadulterated bliss! We ate our fill, and then Patty said she'd made a special treat for us. She left, and she came back into the dining room with a huge apple pie. My brother and I thought we had died and gone to heaven.

I need to stop and explain something. When the state prepares a meal for you, there aren't any surprises. There is what they call a standard menu, and they never deferred from it unless some fat cat congressman or senator showed up for lunch or dinner. This standard menu is mundane as all get-out. To eat the same menu day after day, week after week, gets disgusting. Even worse, we had to eat green eggs. How do you get green eggs? Say you have about eight hundred kids to feed and the menu says scrambled eggs. Add two eggs for every child and adult and you come up with some very tired chickens. The state in their infinite wisdom started thinking how they could lower food costs. Lo and behold, powdered eggs came to the scene. Divide the total number of real eggs, and replace them with powdered eggs, and you should be able to catch my drift. This isn't where you get green eggs though. Where you get green eggs is when you get cheap, and start adding more powder than eggs, thus creating lower food costs for the state. The head cook for the dining hall had a budget, and the school was always trying to lower that budget. They did, and we had to eat green eggs. Not totally green, but green nonetheless!

Back to Patty and that gorgeous apple pie. When she brought the pie in, I really thought I had died and gone to heaven. There was more—homemade vanilla ice cream. My tongue was slapping my brains silly, trying to get at that pie. Patty served it up, and said we could have more if we wanted it. Folks, that was the worst thing she could have said. In nothing flat, my brother and I ate our piece of pie and ice cream. Do you know what happened next? I got the worst headache. Patty and B.M. were laughing their heads off, and we were sitting there not knowing what to do. After a small time the pain left, and she served us up another piece of pie. This time Jon and I ate each bite very slowly, and we enjoyed each one. Patty then asked if we'd had enough, and I can tell you, I was full. She asked us to come help her with the dishes. Jon and I went to the kitchen with her. She washed, I dried, my brother put the dishes on the counter in a neat, orderly pile, and then Patty put them away.

After dinner we went out on the front porch of their home and sat and talked about all sorts of things. B.M. asked us about our family, and if we had anyone special in our lives. We said no, and he asked us a strange question. He asked us if we would like to come and stay with him and Patty. Folks, I told you before, I thought I had died and gone to heaven. When B.M. asked that question, my heart stopped, and I do mean stopped. I couldn't believe my ears. The dream of possibly having a home was something more than I ever realized. I was as happy as a little thirteen-year-old boy could be. From the look on my brother's face, he was delighted too. I think everyone present was happy. B.M. said he and Patty had talked about it for some time. They had everything they wanted, except there was one thing missing in their lives—children. I was delighted that we might finally be getting our own home. Little did I know, this dream would be short lived.

53

B.M. took us back to school that night and told us he would start the process to try and adopt my brother and I. He asked us to be on our best behavior, and we said we would. Jon and I thought for the next few weeks that everything would be fine, and we would soon be heading for a family of our own. Little did we know, this feeling would be short lived. Everyone out there thinking this sad story was about to end on a high note and have a happy ending has another thing coming. Much to our dismay, the state had a very stringent child adoption program and they said B.M. and Patty didn't qualify to adopt my brother and I. They weren't well-off enough. Because of B.M.'s bill structure they figured he couldn't afford adopting us. This made B.M. madder that a wounded bull. He challenged the state to prove to him he and Patty weren't fit to raise us. The state replied, they didn't have to, these were the guidelines, and they existed to protect the kids' welfare. Imagine this—my brother and I almost died twice, and the authorities were now concerned about our well-being? Give me a break! In the fewest of moments, my life came suddenly crashing down on me.

I was mad, bewildered, and confused. I didn't understand and didn't want to. For my brother and I, the state's decision was something that would turn me against everything they stood for. I was hurt by their decision-making process. There would be nothing they could do to change my opinion of them, as I had before. A large part of me died that day, as it did with my brother. Our dreams had been shattered, and there was absolutely nothing B.M. and Patty could do. They hired an attorney to assist them in the adoption process, however it was for naught. He was unsuccessful and the adoption process stopped. Now, you might think it stops there. Wrong again. The state, in its infinite wisdom, shared the belief that Patty and B.M. shouldn't have any further contact with us and prevented them from any future contact with us. My brother and I were taken out of the laundry. We were assigned to the kitchen, where we would remain for the next year. I couldn't believe my eyes and ears. I always believed we would someday find true happiness. After this event, I stopped believing. This was the last time I remembered being happy for a long period in my life. The state's decision was one nobody understood. There were a lot of people who knew about our adoption process hearings. They were as bewildered as we were, but no matter what they said, nothing changed our feelings. Both parties felt it was a huge miscarriage of justice.

CHAPTER 7

We'd all like to believe everyone has a right to find happiness no matter what the cost. I thought so; however my brother and I seemed to get into more and more trouble after this incident. It looked as if we didn't care anymore! Who could blame us? Our purpose for being happy had taken a dramatic and tragic twist. Neither one of us knew what to do. Each time we got into trouble, we didn't care what the punishment was. We'd just do the time and move on until the next incident, then do the time all over again. B.M. caught wind of this one day and paid us a visit as he was leaving campus. He saw us walking down the highway as we were going to the store. He stopped to ask if we wanted a lift.

We weren't supposed to be seen with him or even near him or, if we were caught, he could lose his job, and it would mean more punishment for us. We didn't care, so we accepted his offer and got in. He asked us where we were going and said he would take us there. As he drove us to the store B.M. asked us how we were. It had been awhile since we'd seen him and he was concerned! He mentioned he'd been hearing some bad things about us and told us he was surprised. He said he thought we were better than that! He told us, if we gave up, we would be letting the state think their decision was the correct one. B.M. challenged us that day as we rode with him to the store. He made us aware there would always be times when you're going to get on a horse and get bucked off. He told us that the true men in life are those who, when they get thrown off and hit the ground hard, get back up, dust themselves off, and try again, no matter how hard it seems.

Jon and I didn't have much in our lives, but our most valuable possession was our pride! B.M. was opening our beliefs to possibilities and trying to structure us in a positive direction. I learned something valuable from him that would stick with me for the rest of my life. We accepted his challenge, and Jon and I set out on a new course that would lead us away from the disappointment of life and project us forward to events that would forever hold purpose and meaning in our lives. We would still suffer through tragic events, some more hurtful than others, however B.M., in his short metaphor, set us straight with a clear-cut plan and purpose toward the development of our futures. We couldn't and wouldn't let the state win. To let them would be allowing them the knowledge they were right and they knew what was best for us; we knew better!

Jon and I moved on, becoming teenagers, getting smarter and harder as we moved forward with our lives. Little things didn't hurt us any longer, as they had in the past. We used each moment we could to harden our hearts and spirits to the cause we knew lay ahead for us. We were still little boys, but we were now fourteen and getting into the girl stage. We each had girlfriends. We relished the time we could spend with them to talk and learn about the mystery of girls and boys. If you thought we were having trouble with the boys, imagine the problems we discovered the girls were enduring on the other end of campus. Jon and I learned that the nightmares we were accustomed to were nothing compared to what the girls were going through. I have to caution you about what you are about to read. This part is difficult to think about and even harder to write.

You see, while the boys were being attacked by our own kind, getting beat up and abused on our end of the campus, we had absolutely no clue as to the living hell that existed for the girls some half a mile away. Most of the girls on that campus were sent to our school because most of them got in trouble at home or were from an abusive family, where they were attacked by in-laws or other adults. I found out later that a large majority of them had been physically or sexually abused in one form or another. There were almost five hundred girls at our school at one time or another. They ranged in ages from seven to eighteen. As you might guess, my brother and I were shocked. We heard stories about some of the girls being attacked and raped by the very counselors assigned to help them. We asked what the girls could do about it. Their reply was, absolutely nothing. There wasn't anything anyone could do. No one listened, and for a while, no one cared or believed.

This is crazy, you're probably telling yourself. Correct, however imagine what the older boys in our school were going through when they found out what was happening. Some of them had sisters at this school. I didn't realize this for awhile, and it shocked me when I discovered it—even more so when I would find out my two sisters were headed our way. It seemed our blessed mother had finally gotten her fill of them. I learned from our counselor that our mother was in the process of getting them out of her life, as she had my brother and I. I didn't know what to do. For the first time in a long time, I was confused and bewildered beyond belief. This put a kink in my armor, so to speak. My thinking and planning wasn't set up for this kind of problem. I was confused this time, but good!

Now, if the girls were having problems like this most of the time, you could imagine why we had an infirmary on campus, I heard and saw plenty going on whenever girls were attacked. They would do drastic things to themselves to try and take their own lives. Some were successful, some weren't. You always knew something was up when you heard an ambulance going to the girls' end of the campus. We wondered who was on their way to the hospital. Some girls came back, however others didn't. For those who didn't, I always wondered where they were and what eventually happened to them. If you got too curious, and asked too many questions, you were told to mind your own business. This was hard when it was a member of your family, as some of the other kids had to deal with. For a short period, I wasn't that concerned. When our sisters arrived, it became my turn to worry.

I eventually found out that the girls who survived the attacks became constant prey for the counselors. They simply stopped fighting back. From their standpoint, what was the use? If no one would protect them, why fight? It became real for me, when the girl I was dating was attacked. I was told she'd been attacked by a counselor. No names were used, however I found out later who it was. There was absolutely nothing I could do, nothing! The girl in question had done nothing wrong. She'd caught a certain counselor's eye and he had his way with her. I haven't any idea what happened to her. I was told she left campus one night and never returned. I asked her counselor where she was and if she was okay. He told me to stop asking questions and to mind my own business! Her counselor was a man, as all of the counselors at this school were. Does that strike you as strange as it did us? I haven't the foggiest idea why this was. In my entire period at this school, this never changed. You might think that someone, somewhere, in the state department of children services, would have found this alarming and change things. They didn't!

I learned to not ask too many questions after that. You didn't if you knew what was good for you. Some of the girls got pregnant; however the state had a discreet way of taking care of these misfortunes. They would send the girl in question home to stay with grandparents or other family members. The state would pay for the birth of the baby and a year's child support. I haven't any way to prove this. It is only what I heard from the grapevine, but I've learned that our grapevine and the network of this school were hardly ever wrong.

Jon and I learned to leave things alone, especially those we couldn't control. However, when it involved family, it was different. When my oldest sister was attacked and sent home to reside with her grandmother, this became personal. It was now my business. When the news broke and everyone heard she was pregnant the school said she'd been impregnated by a football player. I knew differently. My sister told me who her attacker was; however there wasn't anything I, nor anyone else, could do to prove it. As for the football player, he later married her to prove his undying love for her. I found it strange that the school would send out lying messages to the student body to inform us differently, especially when some of the students concerned were still on campus. Alarming, isn't it? And very strange. However, we got used to strange things happening on campus. As might be expected, everyone lost respect for the counselors and anyone who might have anything to do with administration. It was one huge, cruel joke!

As for everything that happened on campus, you had to be prepared to accept anything, at any time, as Jon and I learned when B.M. and Patty tried to adopt us. We learned to expect the unexpected, when it came to the state. If you think you can figure them out, think again. Their screwy system changed constantly. It seemed, from our point of view, that the only thing that mattered to them was making money off the kids and our ability to perform work for them.

Remember when I told you about the huge farm, and the produce grown and harvested there? There were some four to five hundred acres of farm land, where tomatoes, potatoes, corn, squash, cucumbers, and other vegetables were grown. None of these products were used to feed the kids on campus. During my junior year, in a sting operation by the state department, we discovered the produce harvested on campus was packaged and sold by the state. We never ate anything from what we harvested on our farm, except for tomatoes. Everything that was harvested, canned, and packaged by wards of the state was sold to private companies in the area.

The only product that went to the kids was the milk from our dairy herd. As for the pigs and beef, I can't remember seeing any meat from them going to our dinner tables.

We had other problems as well. I can remember my first involvement with drugs. We were like any school in the neighborhood. With children discovering there were drugs to get high on, there were always some who were stupid enough to try them!

Now, before I go any further, let me make one thing perfectly clear. My brother and I never tried any drugs. Not ever! I'm very emphatic about that, for reasons I will make apparent later!

I remember we had everything on campus that anyone could want to get their hands on—marijuana, PCP, heroin, cocaine, and alcohol. How did the children get these? We had access to anything we wanted, by walking to the highway stores almost a mile away. There was always someone who had what we wanted. When I say we, I mean the teenagers on campus. We could come and go at will, as long as we had permission from our house mothers. There was always someone willing to deliver the goods. All that was required was to have the money. If you did, you could get anything you wanted.

There are moments that stick out in my mind and haunt me, memories as haunting as a freight train screaming down the tracks about to ram into a bus full of children sitting on the tracks, with no escape. I had one of those moments on a warm Saturday afternoon when everyone was outside playing football. We were having fun, not knowing the sudden and heart-stopping tragic event about to transpire. It would change many of our lives drastically!

There was this boy in our dormitory, who was an honor student, and no one ever suspected he was using drugs. I'm certain that if you asked anyone in our dormitory, or in his high school classes, they would tell you it was crazy to even associate him in the same sentence with drugs. This boy—we will call him Jason—was smart, as smart as any student on campus. However, he started using a drug called PCP. It changed his whole existence in the twinkling of an eye. Jason was on this drug, how long no one knew. He took one dose and went berserk, running out of the dormitory and out into the yard. Everyone who saw him suddenly stopped, and just looked at him in amazement. This was so weird. You see, Jason didn't like athletics. He never ran for any reason. Even if it was raining, he would take his time and get wet. He just didn't like to run or rush anything. This is why everyone stopped what they were doing and stared at him in amazement. If we'd known he was high, we probably would have done something. But we didn't. No one noticed the strange transfixed look on his face either.

Jason ran around for perhaps five or six minutes. Then he rushed up to the street and stopped at the edge of the roadway. He put his hands on his hips, looked down the street, first to his right, then to his left. What he did next haunts me to this day. Jason spotted a large concrete truck approaching from his left, some seventy yards down the street. In the blink of an eye, he jumped out in the road, pretending to be Superman, thinking he could stop that truck. I don't know if the driver of the truck ever saw him, but he knew he'd hit something, and he stopped as soon as he heard our screams. It was too late for Jason. Folks, I heard the most sickening thud I've ever heard. Jason never made a sound, that truck took him from us in a twinkling of an eye. I haven't been able to forget the sound of that truck crushing his body as if he were an aluminum can. It's something one never forgets, especially when you see it for yourself. You know something? It wasn't right!

When they examined Jason's body in the morgue, they discovered he had been using PCP and listed it as the cause of his actions. Jason left behind a younger brother that day that also witnessed his demise. It hurt more people than anyone could ever imagine. The superintendent of our school called a meeting for all students twelve years and older and explained what happened to Jason. He explained to us about the use of drugs and what they could do to us, should we choose to take them. For me, he didn't have to say a word. I saw firsthand what drugs had done to Jason, and it was etched in my mind for eternity. I would never use them, and I made sure Jon didn't either.

I use this example to illustrate to my own children what drugs can do to anyone who uses them. It worked. As far as I know, my children have never used drugs, in my house or anywhere else. They know my position—if I found they were using anything, they knew what would happen, and nothing else needed to be said. I was one of the lucky parents. Others I'm sure can't say this!

I had a personal experience sometime later in my life. I had a headache and didn't want to go to the infirmary, so I asked around if anyone had any aspirin. One of my friends had a powdered aspirin and gave me one to take with some water. He thought he would play a joke on me. For him, it was a very bad move. He waited until I had taken the aspirin and asked me if I knew what I had just taken. I told him it was the powdered aspirin he just gave me. His reply got him hurt. He jokingly told me he had given me cocaine, and I was about to get very high. I went berserk and started beating this boy about his head and shoulders as hard and as often as I could. I had only one thought—if I went crazy I was going to make damn sure that if I got hurt, someone else was going to join me. After about ten blows to the head, one of his friends pulled me off him and said it was a joke. As far as I was concerned, this wasn't a joking matter. I let him and my friends know it. I let everyone know that day that if you gave one of the twins anything of a drug nature, to get away as fast as they could. If I found out, some-one was going to get hurt. I think you can guess that type of joke wasn't played on me again. I made my stand and haven't changed to this day.

CHAPTER 8

Everyday at school, Jon and I seemed to learn something new. Sometimes in a good way, sometimes bad. Jon and I were now fourteen years old, we were maturing, coming of age, so to speak. We went through the same hardships that other fourteen-year-olds go through. The only difference was, we weren't allowed to make many mistakes without paying a heavy price! We always seemed to find trouble, and when we didn't, it found us!

Being a teenager was hard work! At this particular school, we were always being challenged, if not in the knowledge category, in being downright tough. It seemed I was always getting into fights with someone. If it wasn't a matter of opinion, it was about proving who was stronger. I wouldn't let anyone pick on Jon. When others did, I had to fight to keep them from hurting him. This seemed to happen almost everyday, and after a while I got pretty good at mixing it up. I joined the boxing team, and after being on the squad awhile, I discovered I liked boxing. I got to be pretty good, and those around me started respecting me. There were always exceptions. I would have to fight, and these fights brought dire consequences! When we were caught by our house parents, we would be punished—sometimes by paddling, sometimes by having to do extra work. I understood, and if I was going to get punished, I made sure it wasn't for just anything. I wasn't stupid, but I realize now, I was downright crazy! There were times I bit off more than I could chew and I would get the crap beat out of me. I gave as good as I got and I made sure if they came back for more, there would be a price to pay! I never let anyone get off easy. In our place and time, it wasn't done and even your enemies respected you to some degree.

I came to realize one important fact in these fights. I hated to lose, and I didn't like being rejected or told I was wrong. It was like a time bomb going off in my mind. I came to a point where I set a standard for myself—if I was wrong, I corrected the problem and moved on. However, the rejection part was something

I couldn't deal with! That part was something that hurt and made me pull in to myself and away from other people. I've since become thick-skinned, and I don't let things control me as much; however the pain of being rejected still hurt something awful. I began to understand that in my earlier years, I didn't know rejection for what it was. When I became aware of it, everything we had known and experienced up till then had a form of rejection to it. I became fixated by this. It controlled me. The only thing I discovered that worked for me was to walk away from it. When rejected by anyone or anything, I walked away, more from the hurt I knew would come. The pain, I could endure. It wasn't pleasant, but I could endure! What greater example of rejection was there in my life than our parents rejecting us and sending us away!

There was another way I learned to handle this emotion. It was trying to turn the negative into a positive. If someone made fun of me—the way I was dressed, the way I looked, or whatever—I laughed and walked away. Did it hurt? Believe me, it did! Sometimes I hated them, and everyone who made fun of me, but it became a turning point in my life. I became stronger for it. I fed off the hate—it consumed me and made me angry at everyone and everything. This emotion came with dire consequences; however rejection was something I couldn't handle. I wouldn't let them have a second chance to hurt me. I would close them off from my mind and form a mental wall, which shielded me from the potential hurt and pain. This is harder to do than say. As teenagers, we had many people in our lives whom I didn't agree with. I had to be very selective as to whom I could shield myself from.

62

You're probably thinking that I didn't make a lot of friends! You're right, however, I made my friends my way—and it was my way or nothing. I had very few friends; however they were loyal to me and I to them. Today, as I look back, I was wrong, but it worked for me. Today, at a ripe young age of fifty-two, I have no friends in life. I have acquaintances, children, and business associates, but no friends. I can't bear to trust myself to let things go. It has cost me plenty; however I'm meddling now and need to get back to our story.

I worked hard to try and build my brother and myself up to a point where we respected ourselves. The state didn't do a good job at building self-esteem. If they wouldn't, who would? Jon and I went forward with our lives. Little did we know, we were soon to have other problems thrust into our lives. I told you earlier that our sisters joined us on campus. When the older one, Marie, was attacked by a counselor and became pregnant, she was sent home to our grandmother's. I became so filled with hate after this incident, I made it clear to everyone, should anything happen to my other sister, I would have my revenge. It didn't matter who, how old they were, or what measure of social status they held—I would do what I saw fit to hurt those responsible, should they harm anyone in my family. You might say I made my stand. I made threats, some severe, and my sister was soon removed from campus and sent home to our grandmother's. I'm sure it wasn't from any of my threats, but I thought I had won! I was incredibly wrong.

Remember the boy who almost beat my brother to death? Well, guess who showed up on campus one eventful day? That's right! I didn't know it at the time, however he'd been on campus almost a week when I discovered this. I was alerted in class by one of my friends. This boy discovered Jon and I were there as well. He'd been asking questions about us. It seemed strange to my friends when he started asking about us, especially from a new kid on campus! He also suggested to my friend he wanted to hurt Jon some more. When my friends heard this, they alerted me to his intent. The only problem was, they didn't get to me soon enough! This boy found my brother, cornered him, and began beating on him. I was in the middle of a boxing workout when one of my friends came to the gym and told me what was going on. I didn't wait to change and tore out of the gym on a dead run. I said I would have my revenge some day. Today was payday, the day of reckoning had come. I was about to make damn sure this boy paid for his actions and would never forget my face!

From the time I was little, I always knew I could run; however this day was something special. I couldn't remember running faster than I was at this moment. It must have been the sense of urgency. I knew my brother was in trouble. I knew I had to get to him quick! I was told they were near the cafeteria, so I ran as fast as I could to get there. From a distance I could see the boy standing over my brother, hitting him repeatedly. Jon was curled up in a ball, trying to protect his face and head as best he could. I knew I had to get there quick, so I gave it all I had. No one alerted the boy of the trouble that was coming and for good reason. They knew they would pay if they did. They knew the price and the rules that existed on our campus—if you hurt one of the twins you had better kill the other, because I was bound to make them pay. I was closing the distance now and was no more than twenty yards from my brother when I noticed blood on his face. If you can't stand violence, you might want to skip the rest of this chapter.

When I saw the blood, I don't know what happened to me. Every part of me I knew that was good seemed to fly away. The only part that was apparent now was sheer, unbridled hatred. I ran at this boy with the intent of delivering major pain! When I was seven or eight feet from him, I screamed as loud and as hard as I could. He turned to see what the noise was, and I will never forget the look on his face! He knew he had made a huge mistake by attacking Jon and the expression on his face was not only one of shock, but also one of knowing a price was about to be paid that was something he wasn't prepared for!

This boy had grown since his first attack on Jon, and was about a foot taller than me. It didn't matter! I hit him as hard as I could with my right hand, and he went down. That made things even. I got on top of him, and started beating the living hell out of him! It seemed for an instant all the hate and torment I'd felt and had bottled up inside me for so long, surfaced at that exact moment! I was giving to him exactly what he gave to my brother five years earlier. He never got up. I hit him over and over again, and soon his hands fell away and he stopped moving. I didn't care. I was blind with rage and kept on hitting him. Every so often I would look up and see Jon out of the corner of my eye still lay-ing there and not moving. It made me even angrier and I resumed my attack on him even harder!

Before I realized it, two of the cooks from the kitchen came out to pull me off of him. I hadn't had enough. I wanted more, and I turned on them! Finally the other cook grabbed my arms and yelled at me to calm down. I couldn't, for this was blind rage. I wasn't satisfied. I hadn't had my revenge. All I wanted at the moment was to strike back—to hurt this boy and punish him for what he had done. It was a good thing for me the cooks were there. I almost killed that boy. My first punch broke his jaw, and my other blows knocked out seven of his teeth and broke his nose and face in a couple of places. When the authorities got to the scene and discovered the damage of the situation, they called an ambulance and sent him and my brother to the hospital. That boy was in intensive care for one week. Jon was messed up pretty good and was hospitalized for quite a while. As for me, I didn't care what happened. They could do anything they wanted to me. I'd finally had my revenge. I spent six months in the detention unit on campus; however it didn't matter. If the boy died, I wouldn't have cared less.

Jon spent three weeks in the hospital. When he got out, there wasn't anyone around to protect him, so he ran away from school. I was locked up, so he ran away from what he thought might come. They caught him in Florida. He told me later, he was about to soak his feet in the ocean when the shore patrol picked him up and discovered he matched a bulletin of a run-away from Tennessee. They locked him up, notified the state authorities, and they brought him back, where he joined me for the last four months in detention. He had protection with me. No one would harm him while I was there.

As for the boy I beat up, well vengeance is sometimes bittersweet. Sometimes there is a God. The state, in some mysterious way, discovered this boy was the same one who had almost killed my brother twice. They talked about it for a while and made up their minds that justice had come back and struck one blow against him. They also discovered, from the investigative reports that ensued, that he had done the same to about ten other kids at schools where he'd been. He was transferred to a detention unit after he left the hospital and remained there until he was twenty. He didn't come back looking for revenge. It was a good thing he didn't, and he might have died if he had! I believed in finishing what I start. He was one I didn't finish, and it's probably a good thing. It took a long time for me to settle down. I hated being locked up and caged like a wild animal. I believe when my brother joined me, that was what brought me to my senses, and I began to come around and find happiness again.

For the remainder of the period I was in school, no one bothered my brother and I again. I would be reminded again and again by bystanders who witnessed the fight just how bad it was. They told me I was blind with rage. I couldn't remember all of what I'd done to that boy. Only the stories from others around the scene is how I remember things. I really don't remember anything after that first punch; however I did know one thing—my first punch was a good one!

Folks, I'm not a violent individual. I learned that there are moments in life when you have to take care of yourself, because otherwise you'll get run over and abused even more. I fought to keep the peace within the area I was raised. Had I been in a loving, caring environment, where there was love and structure to guide me through the turmoils of life, I believe I wouldn't have had to fight as much. This wasn't the case in my world, however. I was brought up fast, and in our world if you didn't protect your position in life, no one else would!

I was visited by B.M. shortly after I finished my time in the detention unit. He told me he had heard about the fight, and came to visit me to try and open my eyes to the seriousness of the situation, and the wrong I had committed. This was one of the first times in my life an adult was discussing common facts with me in a loving approach. It was different, and I understood his intent. I knew B.M. cared. If he didn't, he wouldn't have come to talk to me at all. He asked the house mother if he could take me for a ride, but she told him I was on restriction and couldn't leave the campus. We went for a walk to the farm instead. B.M. and I walked together for almost four hours. We discussed all of the recent events, and he asked me how I felt about hurting that boy. B.M. didn't know about the earlier attacks, and the harm the boy had done to Jon. He didn't care, he told me—two wrongs don't make a right, and striking out at that boy as I had only lowered me to his level. I realized he was right. I was having an intelligent conversation with someone I knew I could trust. It was different, and it changed my thinking about a lot of things. I realized I was wrong in my attempt to seek revenge the way I had. Even though it felt good, it was wrong, and I knew it. I was becoming open to something other than hate—honesty within myself.

B.M. challenged me to try something besides fighting and violence. He asked me to join his classes in school where he taught machine shop and welding. He said I had too much energy, and he challenged me to use it for something constructive rather than destructive. I told him I would think about it and let him know. We walked back to the dorm, and B.M. said something to me that changed my whole life, from that moment on. He told me he had always wanted a son in his life, and if he could have chosen anyone in the world to be his son, he would have chosen me. His reasoning, he explained as we walked, is that everyone born into life doesn't get to choose who their family is, or what type of family they have. Nor do they have the opportunity to change of their own free will. I did, and it was my choice from that moment on, if I would alter my course of life. He said if I stayed on my present course, he and Patty would have to withdraw from the picture. However, were I to change and try to achieve some measure of success, he and Patty would always be there for me.

I was confused, bewildered, and lost. No one in my life had taken the time to talk to me in any manner like this. B.M. offered me so much opportunity to change. I knew then my life was about to change, and I would never be the same. B.M. told me it wouldn't come easy and would take hard work and sacrifice. I didn't have anything to lose. Why not? It made sense, and if B.M. and Patty believed in me, I knew it couldn't be wrong.

65

When B.M. explained to me it wouldn't be easy, he was correct. His challenge came with some strong stipulations, and the first was no more fighting. This one would prove to be the most difficult! He told me if he heard I had been in a fight, no matter what the reason, all bets were off. The second proved to be even tougher. I had to keep a consistent grade point average. He explained that to go anywhere in life, I would stand a better chance using my mind, rather than my fist. He explained that using my mind to think first and training myself how to control my temper, would be proof that I was growing. It would prove to others that I could be trusted. I realized that I had a lot to learn about life, and it seemed to be too difficult for me at first. However B.M. told me there would be rewards if I did what he said, and the rewards would be many! He didn't exactly explain what the rewards would be, and left it at that.

I knew I wasn't an angel; however everyone has to start somewhere. I had to try and find that first starting point. Believe me, it wasn't easy. When anyone tries to change their total character traits, everyone around them seems to take notice. It wasn't long before my enemies did too! In some strange way, they thought I'd gotten soft and tried to provoke me into fights over things that didn't amount to a pile of beans. How did I come to this conclusion? It's funny, when you suddenly find that you're living for a purpose and that purpose is worthy of the effort, you start viewing things from a different perspective. My way of thinking was very simple. I learned one simple rule that has stayed with me through my professional life. Everything in life is based upon common sense; if you view things from this perspective, you'll learn the correct decision to make. If the objective makes sense, then it should be correct. If it doesn't make sense, then back away. Chances are, it doesn't and it's wise to move on. I found that when I used this simple rule, my problems seemed to become easier, and my way of thinking changed. I'd finally found something that worked other than my instincts. I didn't leave those behind. I learned to infuse the two and work them together within my life. It was finally starting to look like something could be salvaged for me!

Jon wasn't left behind in this proposal. He was told the same was in store for him, should he want to grow and mature as I was learning to. The problem with Jon wasn't the fighting type. He couldn't, because of the massive damage he absorbed in earlier attacks. His problem was that his attitude was far worse than I realized. Jon had developed an inferiority complex. When challenged on anything, he'd turn and walk away from the challenge. He didn't believe in himself, and it was tearing him apart before my eyes.

There were times Jon would sit by himself, looking out over the fields, with a look in his eyes that was transfixed and lucid. He didn't share his thoughts with me after his last attack, and I knew something was wrong. It seemed all his will and spirit had been taken from him and trampled in the dirt. As I looked at him while he was staring in the distance, I thought to myself that it should've been me to take the beatings. I knew no one could harm me if I didn't want them to. However, with Jon, he had a huge heart that was broken, and there wasn't much

I could do but support and protect him. I knew that with the new challenges that had been presented to me, this would be a tough one. It surprised me though, and it wasn't as tough as I anticipated.

There is a certain look you can give people who are pushing you to a point that is certain to move you to violence. I learned this, and used it often. I called it "the evil stare." Without flinching, and with commitment, you could scare others into believing you were close to reaching your limit. It surprised me when they backed off; however there were always some who needed to be grabbed, shoved around, or spoken to in a direct manner. I learned to do this as well as anyone; however there were always some whom no one could reason with. Words don't always explain your clear intent. Some will only understand violence! One punch introductions, if you will. This action was always as a last resort. If you hit them hard enough and in the right place, I can promise you, they wouldn't want any more. I had to do this to a lot of people who messed with Jon. They wouldn't stop. It was as if they had an addiction to try and bring him to violence. He didn't fight; however there was one thing I learned that would set him off in a flash. Jon had a certain spot on the back of his head, and if you hit him there, he lost it, and in a flash, you had a tiger all over you. After he finished and settled down, it was as if he reached up and flicked a switch. He would go back to his silent self, walk off by himself to sit under a tree or on his bed, and stare out the window. I was only fourteen, and I knew I wasn't trained to discuss his problems with him, or try to help him in any remote way of thinking. I longed for his words, and slowly, as time went by, he became a distant brother before my eyes.

I'll always remember the fights Jon had been exposed to—seeing him in a puddle of his own blood, helpless and bewildered. I blamed the state for not using their resources to help him resolve his problems. If anything, I knew he was gone, he wasn't crazy. He was searching and thinking for himself. He kept things to himself, but in reality, he was searching for a way out. One day he would find it. I didn't know exactly when, but he would!

Jon and I joined B.M. in his classes. We came to like the subjects he taught, and in no time flat, we moved to the top of the class. Not because B.M. liked us, but because we worked our tails off. We would stay after school to practice and ask questions to try and improve our abilities. As much as we liked the class, B.M. seemed to enjoy sharing his knowledge with us and helping us develop our craft. There were times we were good, and there were times we were bad. When we were bad, B.M. would jump on us something fierce. He didn't like to see us do things wrong. He knew when we were playing around or not concentrating, and when we were we received his wrath. There was something different when we did receive B.M.'s wrath—it was never anything personal. He made up with us every time, and explained his actions to us, especially when we let him down. This was something new for us. Our house parent didn't make up or explain to us why we were being punished. Jon and I talked later in our lives, how if we could have chosen a dad, it would have been B.M. There wasn't a greater example of a fatherly figure than him. We later patterned our own parenting techniques after B.M. It

67

goes to show you how much of an example anyone can have on a child's life when things are done in a loving manner.

Jon and I worked our tails off in class. We excelled in everything. Jon was better in machine shop, and I was better in metal trades. I'd discovered I loved to build things from nothing, creating a plan, working it, and developing it from nothing. Completing it was a thrill, and I would use this in my future. I can thank B.M. for that. Every day, when we finished our regular classes, we would rush over to the shop to begin our next adventure with B.M. It was as if nothing else mattered. We were growing in knowledge, developing a trade, and not realizing it, we were developing fathering skills as we listened to B.M. every day.

There wasn't anything we asked B.M. that he wouldn't discuss or try to teach us. B.M. was special, he was like a father to us. He didn't show his affection around the other students; however when we were alone and we performed something right, which was difficult, he gave us a fatherly hug and a warm pat on the back. It was special when he would come and grab us, put his arms around us, and walk us out the door when we closed the shop. He always tried to build our self-esteem. It was something we needed. He sensed it and he delivered! He was more a father to us than anyone could have ever been, that was special!

I was headed to class one day, and was wondering where Jon was. Jon and I usually were always together, but today I didn't know where he was. I kept looking for him, but he didn't show up for class. B.M. could see I was concerned and blasted me a couple of times for not paying attention. When I finally asked him if I could go and find Jon, he saw the look of concern in my eyes and told me he would make a couple of calls. I knew something was wrong when our principal came into the classroom and asked B.M. if he could see me. Our principal didn't come to our class to visit very often, and I knew something was amiss when he walked into our room and his eyes met mine. His look was of concern. He was about to tell me something I would regret, and he asked B.M. to join us. We walked out of the classroom. He told us two boys in a bathroom had attacked Jon, and he was being rushed to the hospital; it was serious, and they didn't think Jon would make it. The boys who beat Jon up thought they were having fun by beating on him. One would hold him and beat him, and when he got tired, the other would take his turn. When Jon fell to the floor unconscious, they kicked him until he bled from his mouth. B.M. closed class, got into his truck, and took me to the hospital to be with Jon. Upon our arrival, a doctor told B.M. about the seriousness of Jon's injuries. Jon had six broken ribs, his face was broken in the same areas as before, he had a swollen spleen, he was bleeding internally. It would be touch and go to see if he made it.

I wasn't used to praying. I did now. Why, I didn't know. I knew someone had to care, somewhere out there, but exactly where I didn't know. Jon was hurt bad, bleeding internally and the doctors were concerned if he would make it. They let us see him while he was in the ICU ward. What I saw made me cold and blind with hate. Jon's hands were uncut, no abrasions, no bruises. In other words, he didn't hit back. He didn't resemble my brother. His face was swollen and bandaged, and he had tubes everywhere. I was scared that I was about to lose him. The doctor said the next twenty-four hours would be the most critical, and they didn't know if he had the will to pull out of it. That scared me—I knew he didn't, and I thought I'd lost him when they said those words.

If you've never had a loved one on death's doorstep, let me explain the flood of emotions a child feels. This was my only friend in life. My brother had shared everything with me in my life; everything I had was a part of him. To see him as he was confused me, and I didn't know what to do. I thank God B.M. was there! Patty soon joined us, and we sat there and waited it out together. We didn't eat, sleep, or move from Jon's bedside. Nothing else mattered. I wanted to let him know I would be there for him, and nothing could or would tear me away from his side.

You're probably wondering what was going through my mind at this time. Was it revenge? Was it hate, or the anxiousness to get back to school to seek out the boys who hurt Jon, and make them pay for what they'd done? Yes, there were some of those thoughts. I'm human, and I was raised in a violent world where the strong survived by being more violent than the others around them. This saved me from getting beat on, but it didn't last. I used the wisdom B.M. had taught me and tried to sort the good from the bad. At present, everything I saw was bad. I couldn't see anything good coming from this vicious beating Jon had absorbed. It wasn't natural, and if anyone could have found something good, I'd have been amazed! Patty came over to my side of the bed, put her arms around me, and asked me what I was thinking. It was hard to speak, but I told her I was scared. I thought I was going to lose my brother. Patty held me for the longest time, rocking me as if to try and pull me from some of the pain I was feeling.

You might think that when a ward of the state gets hurt and their life is in danger, the state, in their infinite wisdom, might notify a child's parents or potential family, correct? Not with us. They didn't make one call to anyone! When B.M. later asked the superintendent if he'd called our family or anyone, the reply was there wasn't any next of kin to contact—no number, no one. I was the only one Jon had. Remember, our sisters were sent to our grandmother's, and they had left word earlier with those concerned that they were not to be bothered in the future.

It was three long days and three long nights before Jon woke up. When he did, he hurt bad and cried. I felt the weight of the world come crashing down on my shoulders at that moment. I knew then, I had to find someone with answers to solve the hate I was feeling and the desire I felt to rip someone's life out of their body with my bare hands. B.M. knew something was up when I started pacing back and forth. He saw the look in my eye. He knew that look, he'd seen it before; he knew what was on my mind and he didn't like it one bit. B.M. asked me if two wrongs made a right. I didn't want to hear what he had to say at first; however it was his delivery and his carefully directed approach that made me listen to what he said.

He told me he knew what I was thinking. If he were me, he would have already killed those responsible. However, he told me that no matter how good it

69

might feel to extract vengeance, nothing would correct or take away from the fact that I would become just as bad as they were. If I allowed myself to seek revenge, I would be as bad and evil as they were. He stood there in that cold hospital room, with both of his large hands on my shoulders, and he told me, as there was a God in heaven, he would see to it that the two boys responsible for hurting Jon would pay dearly for their crimes. I looked at B.M. I trusted him. He'd earned that. He'd never lied to me before, and the look in his eyes told me someone, somewhere, was going to pay. I told him I would trust him; however I wanted to see their faces and let them know they wouldn't get another chance to hurt us ever again.

A meeting came to pass, with myself, B.M., the principal, the superintendent, and two state police. We met the boys responsible in a large room. If looks could kill, they would have died right then and there; however I didn't say a word. My eyes spoke my message loud and clear, and the boys were led out of the room and to a maximum detention unit in another part of the state. B.M. told me they would be there until they were twenty-one years of age, and then they would be released. B.M. knew one of the state policemen who was taking the boys away, and he asked him about the facility they were being transferred to and how rough it was. The officer told B.M. that where these two boys were going, they would find out pretty quick that they weren't as tough as they thought they were. Time would prove him correct, as I learned later.

It was some time before Jon was released from the hospital. The type of injuries he received were very traumatic; however we could see improvement with each day that passed. Each time B.M. would come to take me to see Jon, it was a learning experience. He constantly coached me into forming a constructive attitude, knowing he was preparing me for the future. I didn't realize his intent at that time; however I realized later that I'm very fortunate for the things B.M. shared with me. He is solely responsible for the type of man I am today.

CHAPTER 9

Jon was released three weeks after being rushed into emergency room. Being in a hospital wasn't exactly the greatest experience of his life. He'd been in a hospital too many times, and his character was as scarred as his body. Jon was quiet for a while. I couldn't blame him for what he was feeling or thinking. When I brought the subject up, trying to feel him out, he'd quickly change the subject. His attack was a closed conversation as far as he was concerned. I couldn't blame him! I learned only too late that Jon was thinking for himself. He didn't want to live in an environment where uncertainty was everywhere, and he needed help to keep from getting hurt, and to be protected from the attacks he knew would come. Jon was creating a plan for his escape, so he thought. He was planning to run away from this madness. His plan was based on the knowledge that if the state couldn't protect him from this environment he was forced to live in, he would live in the environment of his choosing. It might be unknown, but he could see the potential attacks coming, especially if he had his guard up.

Jon waited until he was strong enough to travel, when no one was suspecting what he was up to. The state kept good watch on us, but there wasn't a fence around the campus. All he had to do was maneuver around the guards at night and make a break when he thought the time was right. That time was when the guards ate lunch at twelve o'clock. No matter where we went, everyone on evening shift took liberty in the fact that no one was watching them, and they took lunch breaks 40–50 minutes, or as long as they thought they could get away with it. Now if you're thinking Jon let me in on his plan, think again. He knew I would try to stop him. He kept everything to himself, even taking my last two dollars to get something to eat on the way. To where he didn't know, but anywhere had to be better than this hellhole of a place.

I awoke the next day as usual and went to wake my brother up. Imagine my surprise when I saw his empty bed! I looked in the bathrooms and everywhere, when it hit me like a brick in the head. He'd gone and done it again. The authorities put me through the fifth degree. They asked about a thousand questions, ranging from when I saw him last, to how much money he had—anything that might give them a clue as to where he might be heading. One thing was sure, I knew Jon didn't want to get caught. He was very street smart. Any kid in the state's care was. You had to be to survive.

This was his second time running away from school. He made sure the right clues were left behind to convince the state he was heading in one direction. He wrote in his books about going to see our mom. I knew he didn't know where she lived, especially from where we were. All the same, he left those type of hints. I left it at that. I wouldn't give him up to anybody. I loved him; however I was scared of what might happen to him. I knew this was his decision, and if this was what he wanted, who was I to stand in his way? As the weeks went by, I kept wondering where he was and if he was safe. No one heard anything from any of the agencies. If they had, they weren't telling us, and all we could do was wait it out and hope. Every kid I knew who ran away from school was eventually caught. Some in a day, some in a week; however almost a month went by and no word as to where Jon was, or if anything bad had happened. Occasionally I would ask our counselor if he'd heard anything, and he just shook his head. When I went to B.M.'s class, I would ask him what he thought. He would tell me no news is good news and to hope for the best.

Exactly five weeks later Jon was brought back to school, thin, dirty, and miserable. He told me how far he had gotten. He was in Texas on a beach again, having slept in a lifeguard stand. He was fine until a shore patrol went to the stand one evening and found him there fast asleep. He'd done well, but he was caught with his guard down, which understandably made him mad. The state officials didn't take kindly to his running away. There was punishment to be given. Exactly what was uncertain, but something had to be done to make him think twice about running again. I was in class when I heard from our teacher that Jon was back. I didn't see him until the end of the day; when I did, I'd wished I hadn't. The state, in their infinite wisdom to conjure up a punishment, came up with the idea of humiliating him in front of everyone. That way perhaps the other kids would think twice before trying the same. They shaved his head bald, and every day for two weeks made him walk around in overalls too big for him to fit into. He also had to wear rubber boots that were too big for him. The state authorities put the larger boys up to making fun of him, and told them whenever they saw him to slap him on the head or rake their knuckles on his head. They did, especially when I wasn't around. When I was around, they kept their distance. The state took notice of this and forced me to stay away from him. I was forced to watch him be humiliated every day for two weeks. Did it make me mad? Hell yes, this wasn't punishment; it was torture to see him put through this madness. The state thought they were hurting Jon, but little did they know they were adding fuel to his fire. I began noticing something in Jon's eyes each day he was forced to endure his punishment. He was growing in confidence, and he started staring at each boy that approached him and glared at them when they tried to upset him by slapping him on his head. He endured the humiliation and never cried. Not once did he shed a tear. This upset the officials, who thought this would be the punishment that would break him. When they saw him endure everything they could throw at him, they wanted to do something else.

That's when the principal of the school stepped in. Charlie told them he wouldn't put up with any more. Jon had served his punishment, and for him to serve any more was just torture. He told the counselors that if they tried to issue any future punishment on Jon, he would take it to a higher power. One thing was certain—our principal was a man of few words; however when he spoke, people listened. He wasn't the type of man to screw with. If Charlie said he would take it to a higher power, rest assured it was with the state capitol. He had friends in high places. We'd seen this before, especially whenever anyone did anything abusive to "his kids," as he always called us. He would make a phone call, and a limousine or a Cadillac from the capitol would drop by to visit with the superintendent. When they left, heads rolled, and asses got kicked; however Charlie would tell them, "I warned you!" It didn't take long for everyone to learn who the real authority was at our school. Charlie was the man. If you didn't know it, you would in time, and his word and will were gospel.

Jon recovered from his ordeal; however this one took some time. Eventually, we became tight again, but it took some time for him to adjust to school life again. But I could see that look in his eye. I knew it would be only a short time before he would be off again. When Jon decided to run the next time, he told me where he was headed. He knew I was worried sick the last time, and he didn't want me to worry. He told me he'd discovered a truck stop on the highway to town; it was his ticket out of the state. He knew if he could hitch a ride with one of the truckers he could cover a lot of ground in a short period of time and make the state think he was nearby, when in fact he was far away.

His plan worked again. He left at midnight. This time I was awake, and he came by my bed to give me a hug and told me not to worry. Of course I would worry—he was my brother, but I knew he was going to be fine. Did I want to go with him? You bet, but two boys running away made things slow going and suspicious, so I stayed behind. This way, if the authorities asked me anything I could point them in the wrong direction. Besides there was nothing they could do that would make me turn on my brother.

You're probably asking why Jon was running again. He'd had enough of this type of abuse. It was like beating a dog. You can hit on them and hit on them, then suddenly one day they get to a point where they've had enough and they bite you. Everyone has a critical point where they won't take any crap anymore. Jon had reached his long ago. This time he had an ace in the hole. We were both coming up on our sixteenth birthday. If he could stay away from the authorities long enough, he was going to use his plan to make sure that they never hurt him again. He told me about his plan. I didn't like it; however I knew he was either going to get hurt this way or another. If his plan worked, he would be out of the state's authority in no time.

When a ward of the state turns sixteen, that child can sign up for military duty, if they have a legal state guardian to sign for them to enter. All Jon had to do was stay away for eight weeks and he was home free. The bad side to this was that I would be alone. There wouldn't be anyone for me to talk to privately. I would be on my own. I wasn't afraid of anything. I could handle it, but not having Jon to talk to, or have his presence around, would leave me with a lot of loose time on my hands. I'd have to do something to keep myself busy. However, that would come later. I wouldn't worry about that now, only when the time came. For the present, Jon was away, and he had the state boys jumping again.

If there was one thing I'd learned to do over the years while I was under the state's care, it was adapt to change. I had to—there were always different matrons, supervisors, housemothers, etc., to deal with. If you didn't adapt to the many individuals we faced, and their unique abilities and styles of handling kids, you'd be lost and in a heap of trouble. I constantly had to adapt to the quirks and oddities I was faced with. I'd pretty much seen it all! One thing I learned for sure. You could please some of the people some of the time, however not all of them all the time. If you paid heed to this important rule, one could survive without getting hit up side the head every so often. Even when you thought things were safe, you had to adapt. I'd seen my share of individuals who were assigned to take care of us, guard us, govern us, or wait on us hand and foot. What a laugh! We were the ones to wait on them hand and foot. I realized Jon not being with me would create some problems. I wouldn't have anyone watching my back and would have to be very careful where I went and how I moved around campus.

Trouble was everywhere. Our school had all sorts of cliques—white groups, black groups, Mexican groups, and others who were downright thieves. They were everywhere, and if you weren't careful, you could get hurt quick—especially if someone thought you were interfering with their business—and believe me, business was exactly what things were around the kids.

I told you before how anyone could get anything they wanted, if they had a need and the money. Opportunity was everywhere—all anyone had to do was have the goods. The need existed, and if it didn't, someone created it. I have memories of kids getting drunk, high, wasted, and downright plastered with anything from airplane glue, to fingernail polish, to booze of all types. There was also a market of select pornographic material. *Playboy* and other magazines were always popular. We were boys, and what do boys want the most in life? Girls and women.

We had our share of good-looking girls on campus, and boys were always sneaking to the other end of campus to play around and sow some oats if they could get away with it. The boys here weren't unlike boys at any other facility. We were human, with girls here for the taking. It was only a matter of time before you'd hear about boys getting caught visiting a girl's dormitory. As you might guess, it was forbidden, but it didn't stop us. I remember one particular instance where there were a group of boys who went to a particular girl's dormitory. We were having the time of our lives—yes, I was involved! Suddenly the lookout heard one of the girl's matrons coming. The boys, in a panic, jumped out a three-story window and took off running to the farmhouse. When the matron saw the window open she alerted security. When security was alerted, they called some of the counselors who lived on campus and they set out after us. In a flash, every adult on campus was alerted to be on the lookout for us.

This is where it gets funny as hell. The security force caught sight of some of the boys running to the barnyard and took off after them. You'd think they were after a killer, the way they screamed and honked their horns, waking up everyone. They thought they saw the boys run into our huge barn, so they surrounded the barn and waited for the counselors to show up for the round-up. When the counselors arrived, they brought out a bullhorn and started calling out to the boys inside, asking them to save themselves a lot of trouble and grief and come out on their own.

Everyone thought the boys running from the girls dorm had gone inside the barn, but they didn't. Who do you think came out? It seemed the boys who where caught on the prowl this night weren't the only ones out trying to sow some oats. Girls were also on the prowl! There were six girls in the barn waiting for another group of boys, who didn't show. The boys were late and didn't show, especially after the racket started. So when everyone started yelling and calling out for the boys to come out, you can probably imagine their surprise when they saw these six shocked girls come walking out the barn door with no boys following them.

Those counselors turned that barn upside down looking for boys they thought were inside. It never dawned on them there might be someone other than the boys in that barn. As you might suspect, those girls were grounded in the worst way. The boys in question went around the barn, into the cornfield, and back to their dormitory. One of the boys broke his leg jumping out of a third-story window. The other boys literally carried him back to their dormitory on a dead run for almost a mile. The next day the same boy conveniently fell down the steps in his dorm and faked breaking his leg. Smart thinking in some ways, however just one way to keep the heat off his back and stop the authorities from asking too many questions.

I remember this story so well because I was one of the boys who carried the injured boy back to his dorm. I learned my lesson and I didn't look to visit the girls' end of campus for quite some time after that night. Instead, we conveniently met with the girls from time to time, and our discretion became more pronounced. Anything to keep from getting into further trouble. In our world it was always a game, and everyone played—you had to, if you wanted excitement in your life. However the games we played weren't without risk, as I came to discover!

I told you earlier how there were counselors on campus who took advantage of the girls. There was one particular incident where a rape was in progress. One boy, who was on the prowl that night, stopped the potential rape. Now there is a saying that goes "two wrongs don't make a right." Correct, but the state made the boy who stopped the counselors from raping one of the girls, look like the perpetrator and made him the scapegoat. He was eventually tried and convicted of rape, even when the victim spoke out in his defense. He was sentenced to a reformatory school until he was eighteen.

75

The counselor was awarded a certificate for meritorious duty and eventually raped the girl for causing all the trouble. I was incensed, as was every boy on campus; however there wasn't anything we could do about it. I learned those who make the rules often are the ones who can break them, especially when there isn't any accountability or anyone with enough backbone to go against them.

We did have one girl on campus who was a real looker. When I say looker, I mean she could stop traffic dead in its tracks. The type construction workers would whistle and call out to if she came walking by. Anyway, one of the counselors got it in his head that he wanted this girl. Boy, did he make a big mistake! This girl was as tough as they come. We learned later that she had been abused for years by her uncle and her dad. She finally got tired of it and killed her uncle when he tried to rape her. This was the reason she was in our school. Didn't the counselor read her file and case history? Sure, but he thought he was better, and he really believed he could get away with it. He made his attempt one rainy night when he thought he could hide his tracks. He went to where this girl stayed, told the matron he thought there might be some boys coming to visit that night, and he wanted to surprise them. Little did he know or suspect this little lady wasn't going to hear or abide with anything he might say. He went into her room and told her to turn off the lights and get into bed, he was going to wait in the closet for the boys to show up and catch them in the act. However one thing led to another, and soon there was a scream coming from her room.

When the girl's matron opened the door, this girl had that counselor on his back and was beating the holy hell out of him with a boot, one with a wood bottom to it. When the matron opened the door, she yelled at the girl to stop hitting the counselor, then asked her what had happened. The girl told her she had done as the counselor had requested; however when she started to get in bed he came out of the closet and grabbed her from behind. He didn't know it but this girl could fight—and fight she did—she tore into him like a wildcat and busted him up pretty good. That counselor did everything he could to falsify her story. When he did she busted him up side the head. The matron thought there was something more to the story and let the girl beat on him some more. Finally, when she thought he'd had enough, she asked the girl to stop beating on him and again asked the counselor if he wanted to change his story. After the third beating, I guess he got the message and told her matron he was trying to take advantage of the girl. The matron called the police, and they came and carted him off to jail. This was the only incident where justice prevailed for any attack I remember hearing about at our school. The state, as you might guess, downplayed the whole incident by telling everyone the counselor had suffered a mental breakdown and would be transferred to another facility. He suffered a breakdown all right—around his head and shoulders! What a piece of crap! This was on of the reasons things didn't get any better for anyone after this incident.

CHAPTER 10

Kids at school were mixed up as to what religion they were to practice. The state, in their infinite wisdom, made sure we got our share of good old religion. They invited every form of denomination to visit with us four to eight times a month, with some eight denominations total helping us with our spiritual decisions. There were times we would get a double helping, with one denomination coming in the morning, and another in the evening. For kids who didn't know anything about theology or a correct religious approach in life, you could say we got pretty mixed up! One religion would teach one approach, another would teach the opposite. Sometimes they would directly contradict each other. This left us mostly confused as to what was correct in life and what was wrong. I always believed there was a higher power. I didn't know exactly how to contact or approach that higher power without offending anyone, but I did believe.

It was funny when you asked someone at school exactly how to make peace with God, or how to pray. This was a school where the facts of religion were left to the professionals. You couldn't find anyone who was willing or allowed to point us in the right direction. This, I learned, was meddling. It was strictly prohibited by the senior administrators. So we had to listen to the many forms of religion and make up our own mind as to whom and where we could focus our attention on.

I probably have been led to the Lord some twenty or thirty times before I knew exactly what I was committing myself to. It seemed the services we went to were more focused on numbers walking down the aisle than us knowing exactly what and why we were doing things. It wasn't until some five years after I graduated from high school that I discovered the correct path I was to walk, and the religion I thought best served that purpose.

My focus at the time was thinking about my brother and wondering where he was, if he was safe and in good health. This was why I tried to find a higher power to focus my worries on. As a child I was open to the belief that there was always someone of a higher power, but I didn't know exactly how to contact him or her! I would go off by myself and begin talking to the heavens. It seemed correct at the time. I had watched others pray—they seemed to either bow their head or lift their face to the sky. It made sense that the higher power I thought existed would have to be in the heavens, there wasn't another place where I knew there was enough room. It also made sense that this higher power so to speak had to be living above us. In my own imagination I would seek a place of quiet, focus my thoughts or words toward someone I thought existed, and perhaps he or she might hear and answer my prayers. What was I trying to prove? I didn't have the foggiest idea; however watching everyone around me screw things up like they were, I found myself believing there had to be someone in life who was perfect and beyond reproach!

None of my prayers, as I prayed them in those times of need, were answered exactly as I asked them to be. I was never adopted, received a family of my own, or a mother or dad; however this small fact didn't stop me from trying. I had to believe in something. I didn't believe in the state—they screwed things up more times than I could remember! My faith and hope would never rest upon someone who spread lies and mistruths about everything that mattered to me. Still, I found myself talking to God on numerous occasions when I couldn't find the answers in my little undeveloped mind.

I was concerned about Jon and his well being. I hadn't heard word from him or any of the counselors. I was depressed with worry and guilt that I let him go, and I kicked myself every day for not going with him. I wasn't the one who had problems with life as I knew it. Jon was—he was unhappy, tired of being beat up and abused, and he felt unprotected. He knew there was only so much I could do, and even then, he knew I couldn't fight all his battles for him. His approach was one that was thought out and firm. He wanted a life. Something that had a choice where he could see things clearly for himself. It was something of structure and truth. He felt as I had, that if he stayed much longer in this place, he would either die or be left with no choice other than to end his life. He had expressed to me on numerous occasions his thoughts of committing suicide. Jon didn't feel he had much choice. His life as he knew it had absolutely no future, and he was being beaten down, not built up. He knew his choices were simple—give up, admit defeat, or do something about it. His choice to run away was exactly that. He wasn't about to give up, especially when he saw others at school carted off campus in ambulances or taken away to a mental institution. It wasn't pretty to see someone you knew give up on life and be carted away as an empty vessel, no breath of life left in them, and no hope for the future. I had seen this too many times. I couldn't and wouldn't allow myself to succumb to anyone or anything. It wasn't my nature, it hadn't ever been. I was too much of a fighter. I wouldn't give up, and it has been my driving force until this very day. Jon was doing what he thought to be best for himself. It involved risk, he knew it, and he was prepared to assume that risk.

He often spoke to me when we saw someone carted off campus, and he was always afraid he would be next. I was afraid for him. Jon had a big heart, and he gave much more than he ever received. He didn't ask for much, he didn't need or want much, and he never had much wealth, so when he gave from his heart, it was all he could give. I knew it. Perhaps others didn't, but he always gave his best.

To give you an idea what I'm talking about, let me explain what I mean. Jon and I weren't fortunate enough to have someone to provide us with any subsistence, as other children were fortunate to have. We dressed in state issue clothing—shoes and garments that were handed down by other children who out grew their clothes. We didn't have our own clothes to wear until we were seventeen years of age, when we bought them from money we earned working during summer break. We wore state issue our whole lives. It was embarrassing to hear other kids make fun of us, and hear their snickering behind our backs—especially when the clothes we were given didn't fit us correctly. We became thick-skinned after awhile; however it didn't stop the fact we knew where we existed, and we had our pride—not much, but some, and it was precious to us. We always held to the belief that someday we would own our own wardrobe and dress immaculately. We would in time, but not while we were where we were!

Jon was away from school nine weeks before they caught him. He was returned, and the state came down hard on him. First, they beat the living hell out of him and warned him of the consequences should he try again. I watched, as he took his punishment in stride and waited for him to break. To my surprise, he didn't! He took everything they threw at him. They made him do the same as he had before—wear overalls and rubber boots, thinking this would have a demoralizing effect on him. It didn't have the effect they hoped! When the boys came up to him to slap him on the head, he glared at them. When they made him cry, he asked if that was the best they had. I discovered he had changed for the better. He was tough. It didn't bother him anymore, and he knew he had won. When his punishment was over, he marched into our high school principal's office and asked him to call one of the representatives from the capitol. He wanted to ask them a question. Charlie knew what was going on; he wasn't stupid. He asked Jon if he was sure about his decision. Jon replied, "As serious as a heart attack!" Charlie just smiled, told him he thought he was making the right decision, and wished him the best.

Two weeks later Jon was on his way to boot camp. The last day I saw him, he looked into my eyes and told me not to worry. He would be fine, and he would take care of me now. Jon sent me money every time he got paid. It amazed me, to see support for the first time. Amazing that it came from my brother, not our parents! As with anything good that came into our lives, something bad was most certainly around the corner. I knew it would rear its ugly head in time, and it did when I least expected it! I was in class one day, when our teacher called me to the front of the class and asked me report to the principal's office. I did as he said, and when I entered the office I knew I was in deep trouble.

Someone in the administration office got the thought that I put the idea into Jon's head for him to run away and then join the service. I wish I could've taken the credit, however this was my brother's thinking and I was proud of him for it!

79

I was told I was about to pay a price for thinking I could make fools of them and the state! I didn't have a clue what they were talking about, so I went along with their stupidity! I was shaved bald, and made to wear overalls and rubber boots just like Jon had been. When I walked down the hall, older boys would hit me at the counselor's suggestions. They were allowed to hurt me if they could, and hurt me they did! I could do nothing in retribution. If I did it added another week to my punishment. Did I ever get the treatment from them. Everyone knew I was tough, however no one can beat everyone, especially when you aren't allowed to defend yourself. I was tackled from behind, hit until I bled, and received broken ribs and numerous injuries. Every time I looked up, it seemed someone was coming in my direction to give me their share of grief. I hurt plenty, it was hard to breathe, and I was sore as hell. I lost three teeth and I broke an arm; however I took everything in stride. I didn't let them break me like they thought they could.

I remember walking down the hall in our high school one day and I saw one of the counselors pushing boys in my direction, urging them to hit me. I stood there not taking my eyes off that counselor and grinned at him, as the boys came up to me one by one and hit me again and again. I didn't cry. I wanted to, but I didn't. Never would I let them think they were winning. Was it cruel? You bet, I was helpless. I wasn't allowed to defend myself! Earlier in the book, I said that I had the ability to put myself in a frame of mind and place my subconscious to a place where I felt no pain. This is exactly what I did then. I knew pain was on its way, so I pushed my mind to that familiar place, where I knew pain didn't exist. I closed out everything and stood there, as the boys beat the living hell out of me!

I have no idea how long they beat on me, because when I came to, I was in the infirmary, the doctor was tending to me. He asked me what had happened. I honestly couldn't remember, so I rolled over and pretended to not hear him. That's when I knew how bad I was hurt! I cried out in pain. I had six broken ribs. Those boys beat me until I passed out. I learned later that the principal had heard all the commotion and came to see what was going on. When he arrived, I was bleeding from the nose, mouth, and ears. I was on the floor, not moving. One of the boys was about to kick me when the principal came up behind him and knocked him on his tail. He called security and they carried me to the infirmary where I awoke later.

The doctor told Charlie how bad I was hurt and he went berserk. Charlie wasn't a man to screw with, as I told you before. He went to the phone, called someone from the capitol, and he informed them of the events that had transpired. When he returned, he told me no one would beat on me again. The doctor told him had he not intervened, I could've died. My injuries would keep me in the infirmary for two weeks. Charlie asked me who was responsible—and not the kids—he wanted to know which adults were responsible for this. I was scared, however I figured I didn't have anything to lose, except my life. So I told him about the counselors who persuaded the boys to beat me.

It was as if someone from Hell came down and entered that room. Charlie walked out the door, marched to his office to make another phone call, and waited for the men from the capitol to arrive. When they did, he informed them what had happened. They came to my room, to visit with me and discuss my injuries with the doctor. I'm certain if those counselors could have found a hole to crawl into, they would have! Shortly after the authorities left the infirmary, I heard sirens. The doctor told me it sounded like trouble for someone. The state police had come to take someone to jail. They arrested the superintendent and the counselors responsible for the punishment inflicted on me. Hell, it wasn't punishment, it was a beating. I knew if I didn't have the ability to push myself to that place where I felt no pain, I would've died. The doctor was amazed I endured everything and didn't fight back. He knew then something was amiss.

It took a long time for me to heal from the beating. B.M. and Patty came to see me, and it was all I could do to keep from crying when they walked into my room. The look in their eyes told me everything I needed to know about how I looked. I had bruises over most of my body, and I urinated blood for a week from the punches I received in my back and the kicking I got. It was hard going, but it wasn't the end of the world. I'd been in this position before, so it wasn't new to me. I just knew this wasn't the first time for me to be like this. I was also sure it wouldn't be the last. I expected more to follow! It was normal for me to look at things this way. I'd expected retribution for Jon leaving campus and beating the system, so to speak; however, I didn't expect to receive what I'd gotten.

Now, you're thinking drastic changes will occur, and heads will roll in short order, correct? Wrong again. As fast as I healed, the process and the attack on me was swept under the rug, and everything returned to normal. The counselors who were responsible for the beating returned to school. Whenever I had to report with my counselor to inform him of my healing process, each of the counselors responsible for my beating would stare at me with sheepish grins on their faces. They would point at me with their fingers, as if they had guns, and go "boom." Was I scared? You bet your ass I was. No one, including my counselor, said anything that gave me comfort in that this wouldn't happen to me again. My counselor refused to look in my eyes whenever I met with him. Was I concerned? Nope, I was terrified. I was a child who had been beaten close to death. I felt as if I was the perpetrator. I felt I was the one who was guilty. This is what I came back to!

Shortly after I left my counselor's office one evening, I went to see B.M., to let him know I was scared. I met with him and Patty and asked them what I should do. He didn't know for sure; however he did say he would get in touch with some of his friends to let them know they should be on the watch for mischief from some of the counselors. He told me he would go and talk to the counselors and let them know if anything happened to me, or if another attack came on me, he would personally see to it that they would pay. He didn't threaten them, he just told them there would be hell to pay and they would regret it should anything happen to me! B.M. knew he could lose his job by going to them, but he didn't care. I was proud of what he did. I admired his pride and guts, and I believed I was safe for a while—but not out of the woods by a long shot.

81

It took a while for me to return to normal life. I couldn't do many of the things I had before. I was stiff and sore, and my body would take a while to heal from the attack I'd absorbed. Strange things started happening around me though. Some of the kids came to me and told me they had seen the attacks I'd received. They weren't happy about it; they were concerned. If it could happen to me, then it was only a matter of time until it could happen to them! You might say we bonded. They told me they would watch my back if I would watch theirs!

It remained peaceful for a while; however when things happened around campus, believe me, everyone took notice. There was always something going on. All anyone had to do was keep their ears opened and they'd hear the rumors and the threats that were being spread around. We had our share of racial equality. The boys who attacked me were black. This didn't go unnoticed for an instant. Even in our situation, we had our set of honor and rules. If any beatings were going to happen, the white kids did theirs, and we left the black kids administer to their own. When I was attacked, everyone took notice that these black kids were having fun beating the hell out of me. I didn't know it at the time, but some of the larger boys took notice and in time settled the problem with each boy who had attacked me. There were rules, silent unspoken rules, and everyone abided by them. It was the way things were done. As each boy was attacked, they were told if they beat up a white kid again, they would get hurt again. Pretty soon, the counselors responsible for my attack had a tough time getting anyone to hit me. The black kids backed away from them, and told them they couldn't—if they did, they would get hurt. Now, you're probably thinking, this would be the end of things, right? Nope, things got worse.

When these counselors couldn't get other kids to attack me, they started trumping up punishment and disciplinary action for me to do. When I did as they asked, they would call me to the counselor building, have me come into their office, and tell me to assume the position. What was the position? When there was a spanking or "licks," as they called them, coming your way, you would be told to drop your pants, bend over, and grab your ankles. This happened to me more than my share. They would spank me with a paddle that was three-quarters of an inch thick, three feet long and eight inches wide, with quarter-inch holes drilled into every inch square. I remember them hitting me, sometimes until either I bled or the paddle broke. I wouldn't cry. I would take my mind to that place where there wasn't any pain and stay there until the punishment was over. This came with some dire consequences, especially during times like these! When the counselors saw I wasn't crying, it would enrage them to no end! They would hit me harder, sometimes knocking me off my feet. Then they would hold me, where the blow I was about to receive wouldn't move me. Then, they knew I was getting it good!

I remember times when they were soaking wet from the amount of swings they took at me. As for my little tail, man did it ever hurt. When they were done, I would pull up my pants and tremble when my jeans rubbed against my bottom. I knew then, they had given it to me good. This particular time, they spanked me something fierce. I had a hard time walking back to the dorm. Every night during the school year, we had study hall and everyone had to gather together and do our homework. When I walked in, I couldn't sit down. I was swollen and pretty much in dire straits. This didn't go unnoticed by our house mother. She saw me standing up and asked me to sit down. I heard her call my name; however when she asked me to make myself comfortable and sit down, I guess I looked at her in some way she didn't like. She called me over, and when I started hobbling, she got up and asked me to follow her into her living quarters.

House mothers don't usually ask the kids to follow them into their personal living quarters. She knew something was amiss, and she didn't want to compromise study hall, so she asked me into her quarters. She closed the door and asked me what was wrong. I looked up at her and didn't say anything. She then asked me to turn around and drop my pants. I didn't know it, but I had bled through my jeans, and she gasped when I turned around! I did as she asked and lowered my pants and she cried out loud, "My God, what have they done to you?" She cried for the first time I ever remembered. She called to her husband and her sons and asked them to come and look at me. Her boys played on the football team and were huge, as was her husband. Her oldest son, whom I will call Steve, came to me and asked, "Ron, what did you do to deserve this?" His father uttered, "No child does anything to deserve this!" Steve picked me up and told his mother he was taking me to the infirmary and asked his dad what was he going to do. My house mother answered for him. She told her husband to get her coat and to follow her to the counselor's office. She asked her other son Jim to follow her as well and for Steve to bring me.

We set out to the counselor's office. Steve carried me the whole way. When we arrived, Steve sat me down, and there was blood on his shirt that had soaked through from my jeans. My house mother, with her husband and her two sons, asked the two counselors who was responsible for the damage done to me. They looked at her as if she was stupid and didn't have any right to ask questions of them. They refused to answer her! Her husband moved over to the door, closed it, and asked the counselors again. When he asked them, there was authority to his question! He said, "Gentlemen, if that's what you are, we can do this the easy way or the hard way. It doesn't matter, however we aren't leaving this room until my wife's question is answered! And answering it is what you're going to do! But first, before you say a word, let's ask this boy what happened, and if one of you utters a peep, my sons and I are going to break your faces, but good!"

I told them exactly what happened. My house mother asked me to show the counselors the damage. I turned around, dropped my jeans, and showed them my bottom; I didn't know it but I had holes in my bottom where that paddle had tore through my underwear and pulled my skin off, leaving nothing but raw flesh. The counselors stood there and didn't say a word. My house mother walked over to them and slapped them as hard as she could. "You're pretty brave to beat on a little boy," she screamed at them. "Try hitting someone who can hit back."

I think she slapped them three or four times before her husband stepped in and told her to back off. I couldn't remember her being so angry!

83

She told Steve to pick me up and take me to the infirmary and told her husband to call the law. This time, when the law came, pictures were taken and those counselors were handcuffed and escorted to a police car. Because this was a state institution, the local authorities couldn't handle the situation, so they called in the state police. When they arrived, along with a state doctor and the fire department, there wasn't any way this incident would be swept under the rug. I was rushed off campus to a hospital where I would be protected from everyone and taken care of. Steve came over, kissed me on the forehead, and told me everything would be okay. Just before they closed the ambulance door, he told me he would be my big brother. Let anyone try anything with him around!

I stayed away from school for another two weeks, healing in the hospital. My teachers were sent to the hospital to bring my lessons and books to me, so I wouldn't fall too far behind in my studies. One teacher, whom I will call Mr. Moore, told me not to be scared, things would be different when I returned. He said these types of beatings were over, and the counselors responsible for this wouldn't be coming back to school. They had been relieved of their position. He also told me that the teachers, along with the principal, had met with the superintendent of our school and demanded change. If he didn't, they would speak to the proper authorities and make sure things were corrected, with or without his support!

Did I feel comforted by this? Some, but I had heard things like this before. I was moving to the here and now portion of my life, where I would have to be shown before I would believe anything. B.M. and Patty came to see me while I was in the hospital. Patty cried when she saw my injuries. B.M. told me everything was going to be fine, and things were changing. He told me how every teacher had signed a letter that listed the beatings, and the injustices and problems that existed within our school. They all signed it and gave it to an attorney, demanding the problems to be changed. If they weren't, the letter would be published in the newspaper. They had the superintendent exactly where they wanted him. Things did change—not everything at once—but one by one, each problem was addressed, meetings were held, and questions were answered. If the answers weren't good enough, things had to change. The kids didn't suffer as much after this episode. We still had our problems, which I will address in my final chapter, however we felt like we could call this school home after my incident.

My life changed for the better when I returned to school. It seemed as if a breath of sunshine had slowly crept from behind the dark and dreary clouds that existed on campus. Our house mother became more involved with our lives. She started asking us how we were and if we were having a good day. This wasn't something we were used to. It was something good, and it was change for the better! Life was looking up! School was better. There was one thing which was unmistakable about our school. You could now hear laughter coming from the hallways. Music was played, and children were smiling. This was something that was missing before, and things were really looking up. It was as if we had purpose and drive to better ourselves, and our lives.

Our school took off, and we started believing in ourselves. Before, our counselors had beat us down, not built us up. We were now receiving instruction and spirit at the same time. Everywhere you looked, you could see a new sense of rejuvenation. Kids were now trying to better themselves. We still had our problems. These didn't go away overnight. Some kids had scars—emotional, physical, and mental. As we learned, time heals all wounds, but scars needed cleansing, and children needed to be held, comforted, and loved.

This, my friends, was something only the kids could fix. Before, no child on campus would take their concerns or problems to a counselor. This was something every child learned the first day they entered this school! The counselors were abusers and horror mongers. They were the most irresponsible facets of our school life. To tell them anything would bring more shame or harm. How did we resolve our problems then? We talked with each other and asked what each would do if we were placed in similar circumstances.

I remember horror stories from some of the kids I talked to and discussed problems with. Was I a doctor? Absolutely not, however I had a great ear, and always have. I could reason truth, and scrape away the crap in an instant. I thought it was to be my future job; however I couldn't stand the pain. I didn't know how to keep from subjecting myself to the same feelings each kid had experienced. I knew that to be able to help them, I had to experience the same pain myself. I did this in many ways. I would imagine or feel my way through any incident each kid harbored, as something that was causing them pain and torment. After subjecting myself to their pain, I would then come up with a solution to try and help them walk away from it. Some of the girls told me about countless rape attempts, many on our very campus. This is something you might say I couldn't feel myself. Think again!

In the first chapter, I spoke of a similar circumstance, only it was a boy. I do know and remember the pain they were feeling. I had the same guilt and pain myself. The way I overcame it was by telling myself over and over again, "I wasn't the one to blame, I was a victim of circumstances, it wasn't my fault." I had to tell myself over and over, time and again, until I believed that I wasn't alone, there was someone out there who loved me, and this wasn't love. I would go to bed each night, say my prayers, and ask God to please send someone to love me. This is what I told those whom I spoke with. Sometimes it worked, sometimes it didn't. I tried as best I could. Sometimes I would just hold a kid and tell them things would get better. I reminded each of them that they had to believe in themselves first—no one else would if they didn't. This was a starting point.

Earlier in my book, I spoke about kids who would let their problems get the best of them and succumb to the pain and sorrow that filled their lives. I could only watch helplessly as each ambulance came to take their cold, lifeless body away, and wonder what had gone wrong? Were they weak, or had they experienced something so terrible they couldn't bear to live with the shame and torment that consumed them? These were questions I've felt each and every day of my life; however I can look into a mirror, see my reflection, and reassure myself

85

that I do like what I've become. I'm not perfect, not by a long shot, however I do have my pride! No one can ever pry that from me.

There are many mysteries to life, especially the ways of life as we knew and experienced them. I wish I had all the answers to life's problems, and I could share the answers with the kids I came to know over the years. None of us ever deserved to be placed in an existence where there wasn't love or respect. To place a child in this type of environment only speaks volumes of the sheer idiotic nature, which existed within every institution throughout our great country. We were children, and we didn't ask to be brought into this world. However, we deserved a fighting chance to survive. I would have killed for the love of any adult who would come and hold me each evening, wipe away my tears when I was hurt, and answer the many questions I needed answered. I also knew I wasn't alone with this problem. There were other children with this same need and desire. I knew there were other schools that existed, and there were torments and pains within those school walls as well. I could only hope and pray their pain wasn't as great for them as it was for us.

CHAPTER 11

Summer ended as quickly as it came. Football season was upon us, and we were hoping our spirits would be lifted by our athletic prowess. We were very good at sporting events. This was an advantage we had over the other school we played against. Most of the kids that played football, track, basketball, or boxed, did well because we had no one other than ourselves to please. Sure there were the coaches, and we always had to please them. However, our pride was at stake. It wasn't about playing the game—it was the game of life as we saw things. We didn't like to lose at anything, and we didn't very often! Our football team was the reigning state champion and we were ready to defend our title. We had averaged an unbelievable sixty-three points a game the year before, and everyone was back. Our track team hadn't lost a meet in over three years, and we were the reigning state champion for indoor and outdoor track. Everyone looked forward to playing their particular sport—it was one of the many times when we forgot who we were and the past that haunted us.

When we traveled to another school to play another team, it was thrilling because we weren't allowed off campus a lot, so these away games were very interesting. We got to see how real kids with families lived. It was interesting, to say the least. One of the many things that other schools would do to try to get under our skin and break our concentration was a particular cheer where they would chant, "Beat the orphans." Little did they know, it didn't hurt or break our concentration. It inspired us to unbelievable heights! When they used those cheers, we would turn up our intensity another notch and beat them even worse.

I remember one game in particular. We were picked to beat this team by seventy-two points, in football. There are some people who thought this wasn't attainable, but it was. It wasn't that the other team was that bad; we were that good! We beat them by eighty-two instead of seventy-two. Our coach had us fumble the ball instead of scoring, because he didn't want to humiliate the other coach and his team. One of our defensive backs intercepted a pass the other team threw about three yards from the goal line and walked into the end zone for another score. The other team didn't try to tackle him or run at him, so he walked into the end zone. When our player came back to the sideline, our coach punched him dead in the mouth, and told him he didn't want another score made the rest of the game. Believe me, we didn't. There were seven minutes left to go in the game and nobody scored again. It was something I didn't forget. The other team's coach didn't come to midfield after the game to shake our coach's hand. He thought he had been publicly humiliated. It didn't matter that the cheers they used were to try and humiliate us. It didn't matter, soon other teams tried to do the same—one by one they fell by the wayside beaten, bloodied, and worn out! We attained another state championship for our efforts. My graduating class was undefeated in three sports, three years in a row. Our class set records that remain until this day. Our pride was at stake. We couldn't let anyone beat us. It was personal, it was all we had, and nothing else mattered.

What set us apart from other schools we played against? Our ambition. We had plenty to prove, not just to ourselves, but to the world. Before our graduating class, no state institution—at least in our state—ever won a state championship. We did, in three different sports. After our class left school, no class ever came close to performing as well as we did. We were simply unbelievable. We used our speed in track, football, and basketball, and our toughness in boxing to excel. Perhaps our aspirations for life with a family helped, who knows?

My senior year, our boxing team won the sub-novice, novice, and open titles in the Golden Gloves tournament. No school before us ever accomplished that feat, nor has anyone else to this day. Our toughness propelled us to a level no one could top. We crowned twelve state champions in boxing, as well as other state awards in other sports. We placed six of our football players on the all-state team, something that had never been done before by any school in the state.

All this attention we were bringing to our school wasn't going unnoticed. There were dignitaries standing in the wings, taking credit for everything we achieved. They didn't play the game, or make the sacrifices; however they received the credit. For his efforts, our coach received a new Cadillac upon winning our second State Championship. When we came back from the title game, the car was sitting in front of his house, a bright red bow around it with a note attached, saying "Thank You!" With great accomplishments come great rewards, right? Not for us they didn't. When our sporting seasons were over, our lives returned to normal, if you could call it that.

Attacks still happened to the girls, kids were still being carted off campus to the hospital, and our lives were still lived in horror. We didn't know anything else. We thought with all the good we were accomplishing in sports, someone might try to improve the negatives which still existed on campus. One thing did happen. In an earlier chapter, I spoke about the produce on campus not going to benefit the kids—all of the farm products, vegetables, meat, and so on went to many of the stores in the area. This was being watched carefully by the state.

After we won our track championship, a senator stopped by unannounced for a special visit.

Whenever a government official wanted to visit campus, they usually called ahead to announce their arrival. When this was done, the local press would always drop in to profile how the politician was trying to bring order or benefits to the school. This was good in some ways. The menu would be changed, and good food was served to show how well we were supposedly being fed. However, this particular senator didn't buy it. He had spies on campus for some time, and they uncovered violations that were astronomical. He was about to put the noose around someone's neck!

One fall morning, this senator strolled into our cafeteria and grabbed a tray to serve himself the same food which was prepared for us. This was a shocking event. One of the counselors recognized him immediately, ran up to him, asked him to have a seat, and he would have the cooks prepare him something to eat. The senator, brash as he was, told the counselor he would eat what the kids were eating. Folks, this is where it gets real good!

When the cooks prepared food for as many kids as we had on campus, they would cut as many corners as possible to maintain food costs which were set by the administrators of the state. It didn't matter if the food was edible or not—cost was what was important. Biscuits were prepared two to three days in advance and placed in the freezer. They would be removed when they were to be served for any meal. They were frozen, but placed in the ovens to brown and bake. Biscuits that are frozen and placed in an oven to cook brown very quickly. Some still had ice in them, but it didn't matter. The menu said biscuits were served, and they were served, ready or not. Eggs were prepared with the normal ration of powder. Some would be green when there was too much powder mixed with the real eggs. Bacon was fast-fried, with grease sitting in a large container. When the bacon was finished and placed in a serving tray, there would be about two to three inches of grease in the bottom of the tray. More bacon was poured in the tray for the next group of kids coming through the doors. This left the bacon soaked with grease. Not good, not at all! Oatmeal was prepared hastily as well. They would pour the oats too quickly into the large mixing pot. This would leave lumps in many portions, dried oats that didn't cook properly and too fast. Many times when we had milk it was sour and unfit to consume. Murphy's Law prevailed on this day. Anything that could possibly go wrong, did, in a bad way.

This senator went through line, just as we did. He was served the same food we were, and it was disgusting to say the least! The senator, as any fat cat politician would, brought his personal press photographers along with him. They went through the line and took pictures as this senator went through the line with the kids. The senator was horrified when he got to the eggs. He looked at the cook and asked the cook what in God's name this was. The cook cleared his throat and uttered, "Eggs." The senator asked him again, and the cook replied, "Eggs!" When the senator got to the biscuits, the server made the mistake of dropping his biscuit on the tray. It hit with a thud, as hard as a rock. This stopped the senator

89

dead in his tracks. He sat his tray down, picked up the biscuit, looked at the cook, and told him it was cold. The senator pulled the biscuit apart, and there was ice inside and the dough was uncooked. The story gets better. The senator looked down the line to the bacon tray, and saw what looked like bacon, however it was floating and sunk deep in grease. He then grabbed a glass of milk, started to take a drink, and stopped short. The senator smelled the milk, and it was bad. The cook started to say something; however the senator held up his hand and motioned for him not to speak. The look the senator gave the cook was one that spoke volumes. No words could be spoken that would explain the travesty the senator was witnessing with his own eyes. He stepped out of line, and slowly made his way around all of the tables in the cafeteria.

The senator didn't have to say a word; the look on his face said it all. It was a look of disgust, horror, contempt, and sheer madness. Our cafeteria could fit about eight hundred kids at a sitting. You could hear a pin drop if someone would have dropped one. No one moved or spoke, except the senator. The senator made his way around to each table, and it looked as if the more he saw, the madder he got. He said something to his chief aide, and he wrote something down as he walked. When he had made his final tour, he turned and asked who was in charge. One of the counselors stood up, and answered that he was on duty and in charge. The senator walked over to the counselor, grabbed his arm, and motioned him aside. I haven't the foggiest idea what he said, however he kept asking the counselor if he understood, and the counselor said he did. Then the senator did something that amazed everyone in the cafeteria. There was a new group of kids coming into the cafeteria to be served. He motioned for his aide to tell them the cafeteria was closed, and for them to come back in one hour and they would be fed. Then he asked everyone to leave. The building cleared out in the space of about two minutes. His aide closed the door, and you might say the house started getting cleaned.

The superintendent of our school was alerted by one of the senator's aides and told to come to the cafeteria. When he got there, there wasn't any explaining or discussion. Our superintendent was told in no uncertain terms what was happening and that in time he would be looking for a new position. Our superintendent protested; however that was the biggest mistake of his life. The senator called his aide over to the table, and as we looked in the window observing everything going on, he began reading something to the super. We couldn't hear what was being read; however from the super's reaction he looked like he knew his goose was cooked.

Every cook who worked in the kitchen, every server, every attendant who worked in the cafeteria, was relieved of their duty. In laymen's terms, they were fired. Our superintendent was allowed to resign, to save some dignity for the school. That morning, no more than one hour after the senator showed up, new cooks arrived and started work. Inventory was taken of what food was in the kitchen lockers and freezer and was logged as evidence. When the kitchen opened one hour later, the food that was served was not only visually appealing, it was delicious. We ate like we never had a meal before. It was amazing how one meeting, and one surprise visit, could change everything. The changes didn't stop there. The senator and his aides went next to the cannery, the farm, and the dairy. State inspectors raided every locker and accounted for everything that was stored. They found evidence that the farm hands were sending produce out to local stores and keeping money which rightfully should have gone to the school or state. They found contracts and bills of sale that got a lot of individuals in trouble.

Corruption was everywhere, and it took almost three weeks to get to the bottom of the food situation. Heads rolled everywhere, there were some thirty adults that lost their jobs, and some were imprisoned for crimes that we didn't understand. However, all that mattered was we had good food the rest of my stay while I was on campus. It was strange that something this drastic had to happen to make things change. From our perspective, it should have happened earlier. It wasn't enough, however. Our lives picked up some after that, but we weren't allowed to talk to the senator, nor were there any questions asked about our usual life on campus. This seemed strange—why come in and solve one of the problems when there were so many?

If the senator knew of any wrongdoing in our administration other than the food situation, he didn't show any concern to go deeper and expose them. Soon we realized, this was just a shakeup—they didn't want to clean everything up. That wasn't how things were done. They only wanted to stir up the pot, so to speak. This way the senator looked good in the papers, and he got reelected. Everyone on campus got a good view how politics worked during those three weeks. We learned that when the government wanted change, it was for a hidden agenda, nothing more. New administration arrived and took command, yet the same major problems that haunted us would still be there. It was too good to be true to have everything that was bad be taken away. The state might push things under the rug, or whitewash the situation, however the major problems soon came back. When the coast seemed clear, we became easy pickings again.

When the superintendent resigned two weeks later, that same senator was there for the assignment of his replacement. Pictures were taken, everyone talked as if things would change for the better. Some did, some didn't, and some actually got worse. Everything that happened was for the good of the good old boys on campus. We learned that some things would never change because they weren't supposed to.

We assumed our normal lives and routines as best we could and tried to change as events and rules adjusted around campus. We could see things that suggested corruption and wrongdoing, however nothing could change people that wished to prosper from changes that transpired after the senator's visit! We found out, in a meeting introducing us to the new superintendent, that things were about to get worse.

When changes came to our school to remove the kitchen and farm staff, this was something that was done to institute a new wave of thinking, something that wasn't necessarily agreed upon by the former administration. What was about to be instituted was going to change how everyone on campus was to live his or her lives. These changes were instituted to reflect racial equality. We weren't exactly racially negative. We were raised under the rules of the state, rules that were set years before my arrival and were the mainstay for life, under the state's rule. However, the state was about to change everything. Even if it hurt, it was supposedly for the betterment of the majority. These decisions came with many sacrifices, some good, some bad. When it reflected upon your values and beliefs, it became personal!

One of the first things to change was the amount of minorities each dormitory would be allowed to have. Presently, the state only allowed a certain percentage of minorities to exist in each dormitory. This amount doubled, and in a very short period would increase even further. The next change was something that couldn't be tolerated by anyone. We were told by the new administration that the black kids could date the white girls on campus if they wanted, as long as it didn't cause any disruption. We were raised under the old rules, that whites were to be with whites, and blacks with blacks. We didn't make the rules, and for many years, even the state would strike out at the students when this rule was broken. It was like one of the Ten Commandments—it wouldn't be tolerated nor would it be broken! This was about to change, but not without major discussion! When the new super delivered this news, there was unrest—everyone got downright belligerent! We were all called to the auditorium for a meeting with the new super.

Many of the kids were there as families, meaning some boys had sisters on campus. This wasn't about to be accepted without a fight, and believe me, a fight was what happened! Almost every boy who had a sister on campus stood up and said "hell no," in unison. This caused the administration to warn us that if we didn't sit down we would be punished. Here we were sitting, the state telling us all the values we were raised by over the years were to be forgotten, and we were to abide by these new rules as if we were total zombies with no beliefs or structure. "Impossible," was what many of the boys replied. One boy, whom I will call Bobby, stood up and asked, in a clear and contrite manner, "Does that go for your daughters as well?" The new super turned to him and told him to sit down and shut up. Bobby didn't, and asked the same question again!

Pay attention to what happens next. Bobby was one of the best boxers on campus, as tough as they come. He was also a born leader and no one was about to shove anything like this down his throat without clear intent, or without a fight! Bobby stood there defiantly looking out over everyone, white and black, and asked the question again! You see, this new superintendent had two daughters. They went to the same classes we did. This made the intent of what the state was trying to shove down our throat somewhat different. Bobby was trying to understand if this new rule was something that applied to a select group, or to everyone. When he asked it the third time, the super told him to sit down or be subject to punishment. Bobby stood there not moving, looked at this man and said very clearly,

"There are many of us here that have sisters and family. We were raised with beliefs and understanding, and what you're suggesting goes against everything that we were taught. I believe you need to answer my question—whether this applies to only us or is your family different?" This made the super madder than hell. He directed two counselors to remove Bobby from the meeting.

This is where it gets good. Bobby had three sisters on campus, and one of them had been raped by one of the counselors. Bobby wasn't in a position to do anything about it when it happened. Now he was! How, you might ask? Guess which counselor made his way down the aisle of the auditorium to remove Bobby from the meeting! Exactly! Bobby heard the commotion, and to his surprise, turned to see the counselor who had raped his sister walking forward to remove him. He stood there, grinning from ear to ear, waited for the counselor to get within reach, and when he did, Bobby grabbed him and hit him as hard as he knew how. We all heard bones break in the counselor's face. Bobby didn't just hit him once either, he held him and punched him over and over again! Bobby was having his revenge for his sister's rape. It took three counselors to remove Bobby from the meeting. This was not the end—this, my friends, was only the beginning.

There were other boys in the meeting with sisters on campus. They stood up and asked the same question. The super didn't know what to do, for he hadn't expected this. When Bobby stood up and challenged him, he thought he was a lone minority. Now, however, there was a mutiny about to transpire before his very eyes. Now, everyone in the auditorium was enraged. We felt as if our very existence was being challenged and threatened. That's when the most incredible thing happened.

One of the superintendent's daughters was at the meeting. She stood up when she saw the anger and injustice transpiring before her eyes. She yelled out to her father, "Dad, why don't you answer their questions? They have a right to know the truth, or are you afraid?"

The super looked at his daughter and became aware he was between a rock and a hard place. She yelled at him again, this time challenging him to respond—"Okay, Dad, tell them or is everything you've always told me all my life a lie?"

The super looked at her and said, "No, my daughters aren't included!"

If you thought we had trouble before, when he told us his daughters weren't included, he knew the gig was up. Almost to a tee, every house mother in the place started gathering their kids to take them back to the dormitory. As far as they were concerned, this meeting was over. The administration would have to think of a new way to make peace now.

Peace wasn't to be. If you thought we had unrest before the meeting, it was nothing compared to what we experienced for the next couple of months. Every time a black kid approached a white girl, even to ask a simple question, a fight ensued. It didn't matter if the girl wanted to make contact or not, it was as if hell had come down. Everyone, everywhere, had taken a personal vendetta toward the state's administrative stance on allowing the black kids to date the white girls. What was lost in the whole mix was that nothing was stated about black girls dating a white boy. My friends, if you thought white girls dating black boys was a problem, don't even consider the flip side. To the black kids on campus, this was a quick way to get killed. I didn't get it—one was okay, the other totally unacceptable! You try and figure it out. I couldn't, and the only thing I was happy about was that my sisters were no longer on campus. If they were, it might have been a horse of a different color!

We had fight after fight, and war after war. I got so used to being suckerpunched it was silly. Everywhere you went, you had to be with someone of your color. If not, you got attacked. I had to finally carry a roll of quarters around in my pocket, just to defend myself. I recall one day coming out of the high school door, when suddenly I was picking myself up off the porch steps. When I came through the doors, there were two boys waiting for the first kid to come through. It wasn't meant personally toward me; however it became personal. I caught enough view of the two boys who had attacked me, and I waited for my time to come when I would get a chance and give them payback.

When I say payback, I mean exactly that. I paid each of them back, and then some. It wasn't that I had a grudge, but I had to let them know they didn't get away with attacking me, so I busted a few heads, knocked out a few teeth, and broke a few noses. It's amazing what a roll of quarters will do to someone when you hit them as hard as you can. I received retribution from some of the older, bigger, black kids and I welcomed it. I had to represent myself! They found out I was honest in my endeavors. I didn't start fights; however I sure as well finished them. The black kids learned that if I punched one of their own, I usually had a reason. I tried to walk my own path and didn't believe in marching to others' agendas. I'd seen where that could get you if you did. Sometimes, if you were wrong, you got hurt. The odds were against you. When I started school, the racial balance was about thirty percent white and seventy percent black. When I graduated, it had expanded to fifteen percent white and eighty-five percent black. I wasn't the brightest kid in class; however I wasn't a dummy either. I learned that if you walk to the beat of your own drum, you'll gain a little respect along the road of life. Not everyone will respect you; it's something you have to earn. I learned that if you wanted respect, you had to earn it. How? If I was challenged and I had to fight, I picked the biggest and strongest opponent. I usually got my head beat in; however I gave as good as I received. In time, the larger black kids knew I was different. Some of them thought I was downright crazy. But in time they let me be. When I went after a particular person, they knew the person I was after had probably done something to deserve my wrath.

If you thought the state wasn't watching, think again. They were always watching and waiting for an opportunity to step in and administer their form of justice. We considered their judgment as something worth the trouble. In many respects, we viewed what the state did to us as nothing more than a mere formality—in other words, judgment without respect. We'd lost respect for their authority after the new super's meeting. There wasn't anything they could do to ever earn that back.

CHAPTER 12

I had finally reached my senior year in high school. I hadn't thought I would get this far. It was amazing, to finally be so close yet so far. I didn't have a clue as to what I would become, or where I would go once I graduated. But I was a senior. It felt good; it was something I'd earned. However, there was still a void in my life. I didn't have anyone to share my achievements with.

My brother came to visit after he got out of boot camp. As might be expected, the counselors weren't exactly thrilled when he arrived on campus. The state officials told him he couldn't stay with me. He told them, with respect, that he didn't intend to, he had a hotel room off campus, so they could forget whatever they were getting at. Jon had grown some. He was bigger, stronger, and prouder. Going into the army was the correct decision for him, and he had really performed well. He asked me how things had gone since he'd left. I told him about the beating I got, the senator's visit, and everything that transpired. He was concerned about my welfare and asked if I wanted to join him. I told him I really wanted to do something no one in our family had ever done before. I wanted to graduate from high school. Even Jon hadn't achieved that—he had taken his GED in the army and passed; however it wasn't the same. He knew it would be something special for the both of us. He told me he was proud and would support me in any way he could.

Jon was the only person who ever came to visit me while I was at this last school. In retrospect, in all the schools we were sent to, we'd only had one other person visit us. That was our uncle and I regretted that in a severe way! We didn't receive a card, letter—nothing from anyone in our family, including our sisters. As far as we were concerned, when we had picked ourselves up on the mountain at the tender age of five, walked back to our room, and made a stance that we were on our own, that was the way we kept it. We didn't feel sorry for ourselves. We didn't need to—that was wasted energy—we had work to do, and things to learn, and feeling sorry for ourselves wouldn't help the situation.

95

Jon stayed with me for a week. He took me to my first movie, bought me my first non-state provided sneakers, and gave me spending money for a while. When he said his goodbyes to me and said he had to return to base, we both cried—not from saying goodbye, but from love, something I've only felt for one other person in my life.

Jon was my lifeblood. He was the only family I knew, so to see him get into that cab and pull away was a tough experience. However, as young as he and I were, we discovered one simple truth about ourselves. We were finally men—not just physically men, but men in spirit and heart. No one who beat us, or abused us mentally or physically, destroyed the one simple truth we held on to all our lives. We knew we had each conquered everything we'd faced. We'd achieved the impossible. Sure, we had scars to show for our journey, but we also had the knowledge that we'd won the fight. We knew the battle wasn't won by a long shot. We couldn't exactly celebrate; however we could acknowledge our hard-fought journey to get this far. Jon challenged me to persevere, move forward to the prize, claim it, and don't lose sight of the goal. I told him the day I walked down the aisle in our graduation ceremony, his picture would be over my heart. I would be walking the walk for the both of us. If the state hadn't abused him as they had, he'd have been with me, but I couldn't lament about that now. There was still almost a year to go, and there was a lot to do, so I had to bear down.

When we started school, I buckled down in my classes. I had so much to learn, and I wasn't about to let anything cheat me from my goal. I had some real problems in history class. I had a learning disability, and it was holding and retaining dates. I couldn't remember anything concerning a date from historical events. I tried everything, but I couldn't retain the simple task of remembering dates. I stayed after class one day and asked my history teacher what I could do to help myself remember them. He said he would help me, if I was willing to do the work. He challenged me and told me I had to pass his class in order to graduate from high school. I knew I had to. I didn't have an excuse, so I did as he requested. To my surprise, he showed me, slowly but surely, how I could retain dates, if I practiced one simple task—put them to music. He knew I could sing, and I loved music, so he improvised some tunes, replacing words with dates in history to the music. He laughed his tail off when we had a test in class. I would be in the back of the room, humming the tunes and remembering the dates. In time, I didn't have to hum the tunes, as the dates came naturally.

I went after my vocation as if it were the only thing that could get me through life. I enjoyed this class, and I was the best in everything, I could operate any machine in machine shop and outperform anyone in welding class. In time, it was to be my future, but only for a short period. I would get bored and pursue college. I had a thirst for learning and wanted to learn anything and everything I could. To me, it was a matter of life or death, and I didn't know how I'd put in the extra effort to learn. This, I found out, is what separates those who succeed from those who fail. B.M. taught me that. There wasn't a day in class he didn't grill me. He pushed me hard, telling me over and over again, "You'll be thankful someday, when I'm not around. Learn now while it's easy. Someday you'll have to pay, and you'll be glad that it was me who taught you rather than a mistake."

My life seemed to be passing before my eyes. I didn't concentrate too much on girls. I realized they would be around later, but now wasn't the time. Although I did fall madly for one redhead. She turned my life upside down, and got me into a lot of trouble as well. Especially when I paid more attention to her than listening to the teachers. I did learn that if the girls cared for me they would wait. They had to, I didn't have anything to offer—no home, no future, and no family. I became fixated by this, because it became a turning point in my life.

I realized one day in class what the future was like if you had nothing to offer. Up until then, I'd always had the state to furnish me with clothes, shoes, books, meals, and rules. Some of the rules were good; however I was a realist and rules should have rewards, especially if you abide by them. Did I discover how wrong I was. Just because you follow the rules of life doesn't mean you'll have an easy walk. Sometimes it means the exact opposite. Even when you follow the rules of life, you can and will get hurt. I was about to learn the most serious lesson of my life.

I'd been raised to believe that rules were designated to govern those in life who can't govern themselves. The state saw fit to inform us whenever we broke their rules; however those who make the rules don't always have to abide by them. Simply put, those who make the rules can break them as they see fit, anytime, anywhere they wish. What happened to bring this on? I will explain.

We had a couple of kids on campus that were close to each other. They were in love, more than anyone I'd ever known. The girl's name was Cheryl. She was a bright looking, beautiful redhead. The boy's name was Tommy. He wasn't exactly the greatest looking guy on campus, however they fell for each other and planned to marry after they graduated from high school. The problem between them was that Cheryl was placed in our school after being raped by her father and uncle. In the process, she became frigid and wouldn't allow any male to touch her, including her boyfriend. Tommy was a tolerant, understanding guy. He knew he'd have to be patient in order to bring her out of the state she was in, especially if he loved her and wanted a future with her.

When we went on field events, or traveled away to play other schools, you'd always see them walking together, never touching, but close and speaking to each other, and gaining respect for each other every day. Something happened one day that brought total misery to both of them. The state trumped up a rape charge against Tommy and said he raped another girl on campus. The girl, whom I will call Susan, was raped and said she thought it was Tommy. But it wasn't. Tommy was in study hall, with witnesses to back him up. However, the state didn't allow them to come forward in his defense. The state, in their infinite stupidity, prosecuted Tommy, who was innocent. He was sent to jail for ten years. There wasn't a single person on campus who didn't know Tommy was wrongfully charged. It didn't matter, not to the state. They wanted justice and they got it, even though it was a miscarriage.

Everyone involved, meaning the state officials, celebrated, thinking it was the end. The state had won; however it was a victory short lived. You see, the girls in the dormitory where Susan was raped had learned that Susan trumped up the charge to cover for a counselor who attacked her. The counselor, when he found out Susan was going to the authorities, went to her and threatened her. He told her if she didn't change her mind, he'd return and she might not survive the next time. Her fellow roommates were incensed, especially when she charged Tommy.

Every girl in the dormitory knew that Susan had been raped. That wasn't the problem. They learned the counselor that raped her was still visiting her room. Susan was afraid to tell anyone about it because of his threats! The girls went to her and made her realize that she had to come forward to inform someone what was happening. If she didn't, someone other than her might be next. I don't exactly know how they made her change her mind; however I heard there was some pain involved to get her to open up and tell the truth. They set the counselor up. This counselor was responsible, as we later learned, for raping quite a few girls on campus. Later, they came forward, one by one, and informed the state of his actions.

The counselor in question always made an excuse to visit the girl's dormitory when there were very few girls around. This meant he would visit when everyone was either doing their homework or coming back from the cafeteria. He arranged to be in the dorm when the girls were coming back from the cafeteria. He sought out Susan and told her to follow him to her room. How could the counselors get away with being in the girls dormitory? It was simple. The counselors were over everyone on campus. They were like gods. It was big trouble if anyone questioned their motives. They moved at will around campus, and this counselor wasn't the only one who was guilty of abusing the system and the girls. There were more, however they hadn't been caught, but that was about to change.

This counselor led Susan to her room and pretended to pull a surprise room inspection. This was the way they infiltrated the girl's dormitory. It worked every time they wanted to see or attack one of the girls. This time, however, he was in for a rude awakening. There were five other girls waiting in Susan's room. They waited in her closet, waiting for the counselor to begin his attack; this time there wouldn't be one.

The girls who were waiting for him had planned the event in such a way, where they told Susan to get him to talk about his attacks, make him admit to his attack on her and his attack on others. They informed Susan that if she did as they requested, the counselor wouldn't be able to do anything against them, because there were five of them. If he argued, he wouldn't stand a chance in a court of law, which was where he would soon be.

Susan, upon entering the room, asked the counselor if he meant what he'd said about hurting her should she inform anyone about his attacks on her. The counselor, thinking he had everything under control, replied, "That's right, no one would ever believe a tramp like you. You girls are all alike, you come in here and you parade around as if you own the world; however you have another thing coming to you. I make the law around here. I do what I want, to anyone I want. Who is going to believe you? The law? Get real, they haven't so far; now get on the bed!"

Susan started to get on the bed, then she turned and asked the counselor, "So it was a setup, making everyone think Tommy had raped me, wasn't it?"

The counselor replied, "Yes it was, why are you asking so many questions?"

Susan replied, "I want to try to understand why you're doing this and why you are hurting me and the other girls. There are others, aren't there?"

The counselor stopped and looked at Susan. He replied that he had attacked about ten or eleven girls—"I don't remember; there have been so many, I've lost count. One thing's for certain—I get what I want. Now lay down!"

The girls in the closet waited until the counselor had removed his clothes and got on the bed with Susan, and then they made their move! One by one, they came out of the closet. One of the girls had a bat, and the other girls had belts. The counselor was so consumed by his attack on Susan, he didn't hear anything; however he sure felt their presence. The girl with the bat hit him square in the ribs, and the counselor screamed as if he was dying. He turned in the direction where he thought the blow had come and was struck firmly in the face with one of the girl's belts. Everywhere he looked he saw girls, but not in the way he was accustomed to! The girls laid into him and beat the crap out of him. Susan got free after the blow to the counselor's ribs and began hitting him in the face with her fist. Every move the counselor made was answered with a blow somewhere to his body. It seemed as if the sky opened up and was raining blows on him from all directions. The counselor was a big man, about 6'2", 200 pounds; however there were five girls now hitting him from every conceivable direction. He tried to guard his privates, but he wasn't quick enough. One of the girls took dead aim and kicked him hard, bringing a howl out of the counselor that could be best described as a banshee type of scream! One of the girls had been told to go and get their house mother when the attack began and call the police. The girl did just that. When the first blow was struck with the bat, she tore out of the room down the steps to their house mother's quarters. She banged on the door screaming that Susan was being attacked and to call the police.

Back in Susan's room, the attack waged on. The counselor was now on the floor, getting the hell beat out of him. The girls were incensed. They knew they had to keep him down so he wouldn't get away. The counselor wasn't going anywhere. The first blow broke three of his ribs and drove the air out of his lungs. Every blow he received caused him to cry out in pain. He begged them to stop, saying over and over, "I won't hurt you."

One of the girls, hearing him beg, told him, "Is this how your victims called out to you? Go to hell!" And she hit him again.

Now this whole attack wasn't lost on the other girls who were in the dormitory. Upon hearing the commotion, and the counselor screaming and begging, they came to Susan's room to see what was happening. What they saw was justice, southern style. The counselor was nude, and he was bleeding from some of the welts where the girls had struck him with their belts. The girl with the bat was beating him on the shoulders. Each time she hit him, things would break. The attack lasted only thirty seconds; however to the counselor it seemed like eternity. He was now lying on his belly, hardly moving, not making any effort to pull away from his attackers. There's something to be said for unconsciousness. It was the only thing that saved him from probably getting killed.

When the counselor stopped moving, the girls stopped their attack and took their belts to bind his hands and feet. When the house mother arrived in Susan's room, she was horrified at what she saw. The counselor was naked as the day he was born. She looked at the girls who hadn't noticed her arrival and asked what in the hell was going on. Folks, this is going to be the best example of street justice you'll ever read about! The girls, one by one, explained what happened and told the house mother they waited for the counselor to attack Susan and then came out of the closet and started beating him off Susan. They told their housemother the whole story—how he raped Susan, blamed it on Tommy, and about the other attacks he had admitted to. Their house mother stood there in disbelief with her mouth wide open, looking first at the girls then at the counselor who was still unconscious lying on the floor, breathing very heavily, and in a lot of pain.

The house mother didn't know what to believe. The evidence was apparent. It was obvious the counselor was in the process of attacking one of the girls. She was confused, not really understanding everything she saw before her eyes. Then something happened that blew everything out of proportion. One of the girls in the hallway spoke up, telling the house mother he'd raped her also! The house mother turned and asked who had said that. A little girl pushed forward through the crowd of girls. The girl was no more than thirteen, a frail little thing. She told her house mother how he had attacked her some two weeks before and told her that if she told anyone, he'd be back, and it was his word against hers!

The little girl wasn't the only one to step forward! In all, the counselor had attacked five other girls in the dormitory. A few of his attack victims had removed themselves from the scene by taking their life. They couldn't take the pain and wished never to be attacked again. This was told to the house mother by girls who listened to the cries of the victims at night and had gone to them to comfort them. They described to her how they had found the girls broken, scared, and in shock. The house mother was having a hard time trying to digest everything she was hearing. This was madness; however when she looked at the counselor, it was obvious something had happened. Exactly what, would be left up to the authorities, who had to weed through this mess and make sense of things.

In the background, the girls could hear a siren for the police who were arriving on the scene! When the cops got to the room, they received a story that could be best described as sheer horror. They were told about all of the attacks and rapes, including the attack on Susan, and the false attack Tommy was blamed with. The police took everyone's name, called an ambulance to take the counselor to the hospital, and asked everyone to go to the study hall, where an investigator would make sense of everything.

When everything was said and done, the counselor was charged with four-teen counts of rape and other crimes we didn't understand. It was certain this was one event that wouldn't be swept under the rug by the state.

As you might guess, the police siren got everyone's attention, including the new superintendent. He was in shock when he was informed of the attacks and how the girls had beaten and subdued one of his counselors. He was upset, mad, and confused. How did this happen? He'd read some of the filed reports; however nothing was ever proven, and no counselor found guilty. But the evidence now convinced him there was more to the reports that hadn't been resolved. There would be an investigation, answers were needed, and things would have to change. This wasn't what he signed on for—this was supposed to be a model school. He was discovering he was sadly misinformed!

It would take about three months before a complete investigative report would be presented to the state explaining everything that was discovered. The state did manage to whitewash some of the events. They had to, and once again this was the way things in the south were handled. It might not seem right; however when you find dirty laundry within your own administration, you either wash it or burn it, depending on which of the two is the most effective, and will cause the least embarrassment!

We, the children, took this in as with every event we witnessed and learned from our predecessors how judgment was given. The counselor was detained and charged for his crimes. When the report was printed about the attacks and a trial ensued, the authorities made it look like the counselor was deranged and not in proper mental capacity. What was strange was that the counselor had worked at our school through three different administrations. He was found to be in prop-er mind to counsel us through these administrations, but not now. Strange, to say the least!

Things did change after this series of attacks. There were new rules enforced and guidelines given concerning how the counselors could enter a girls' dormito-ry and girls' rooms. The house mother had to be present, and the counselor could never be left alone with a girl. They could go to the study hall to speak in private; however they couldn't be left alone. This rule applied to the boys as well! I found this to be a travesty. It could have saved me a lot of pain and torment I'd suffered over the years! At least this change came with positive results. Tommy was released from jail, and the state erased from his record all the charges he'd been accessed with; however they never said they were sorry. I found this to be dis-gusting. Tommy was framed. He didn't do anything. Once again, this was the way things were. The state wasn't in the habit of admitting their mistakes. That couldn't be said for the counselor's victims though. Some were gone forever, never to see a smile, or feel a ray of sunshine on their faces. I didn't forget them. I can't remember all their names; however I remember the ambulances, the cries in the night, and their screams. These haunt me to this day. I'm not by myself; there are many others who heard cries in the night, and I was one of those vic-tims as well!

After the trial, the state tried to present an air of truth to the media and kids on campus. We weren't fools. Trust wasn't something the state was worthy of. We abided by their rules, because they were the authority; however every child that stayed within the state's care was tarnished by the events that transpired around us daily. We were scarred and scared. If this type of mentality existed and was tolerated within the boundaries of this institution, what lay in wait for us when we would be presented to the world?

I was soon to find out! We were only three months from graduation. It was something branded in my mind. I knew I had to toughen myself and prepare myself for anything and everything life could bring. I didn't have a clue as to what awaited, but I did know I wouldn't have anyone to turn to. I also knew I wouldn't be allowed to make many mistakes. The price was too high. I saw that every time an ambulance left campus taking someone who couldn't live with their mistakes and even worse misfortunes!

Children are very resourceful. When you think they don't have a clue as to what is going on around them, they surprise you by stepping to the forefront and taking control of events. We were much the same. After the report was filed on the counselor attacks, the school thought everyone would forget and things would go back to normal. They didn't. Kids stopped visiting the counselors, and we'd lost respect for all of them! Many of the counselors who remained were still guilty of abuse and lethal attacks on many of the children on campus. In the state's eyes, they were blameless. We thought there would be a mass exodus of personnel when the investigative report was filed about the attack, but there wasn't! The kids requested that changes be made. We created our own student body, which represented us in how affairs were conducted within the confines of our campus. We thought if a clear and concise group of individuals came forward to inform the administration of our concerns, they might listen. They did, but didn't do anything. The student body was composed of many of the brightest students, who had performed well in class, and in many ways were model students. Their reports were filed; however answers weren't delivered or addressed. Our concerns were probably filed in the trash as soon as they were received.

Our only option was to stop communicating with our counselors. We replied, and went to their office as requested, however we didn't say much. We listened, and if asked if we had any concerns, we didn't give any. Why should we? If you can't trust those individuals who are designated to protect and help you, how could anyone be open and informative about problems that weren't going to be addressed? We ignored them, and openly moved forward with our eyes open to any possibility that could arrive.

School was winding down, graduation was coming, and our lives would be changing quickly. In the many years I'd been a ward of the state, I had fears that I wouldn't make it this far. I'd seen plenty of kids that didn't make it. My resolve was a constant reminder of how lucky—or perhaps unlucky—we really were. In many ways we weren't ready to be turned loose on the world. We'd been taught our schoolwork; however this doesn't prepare you for the tests of life that await

102

when one begins their next journey into the realm of life. I looked at many of my fellow students within my graduating class. I could see fear in many of their eyes. Expectations were high for some, especially those who had loving families and knew they would be given additional guidance and direction as to where to go next in this incredible journey called life. However, there were those like myself, who had no one and knew they had no certainty of what they might be faced with. Were we ready for this next journey? It didn't matter; we were about to be faced with reality, ready or not. It was going to be tough, and their choices would be critical. If they weren't tough, they would wither, much like wheat in a driving windstorm! I was lucky. I already had a job using my trade skills and I had a little income to help me with my next travel into life. I didn't make much and I didn't require much—just a roof over my head, food to eat, and clothes to wear. It was more than some had, but I'd seen this exodus coming for a while and had the sense to prepare. It would hurt many, more than they would ever know!

My graduating class had our finals, and the day of reckoning was upon us. We voted for the selected honors in our class. I received "Most Friendly," something that remains constant with me today. I am truly a loving, caring, and giving individual. It is my strongest character trait! I firmly believe this part of my character prepared me and helped me to become what I am today. I voted with my heart toward everyone in my class, as to whom I thought should receive what selected honor, but knowing that what we did today, and how we viewed each other now, would change as soon as we walked down the aisle and received our diplomas. When we met for the last time in the auditorium, each of us had a little tear in our eyes. We knew our journey with each other was about to end.

We each had comforted, trusted, and loved each other through some of the most difficult moments in our lives. There were some who had model lives, where they experienced nothing that would leave a scar, but there were others who could remember only sorrow and pain. These kids would have a tough road to haul. All we could do was give them our support and try to be there for them, if and when the time came. For some it would be as quick, as they left the confines of our campus for the last time, never to be allowed to return to what protection we thought existed. We all knew things were to change and become difficult for us. Some of us would be going to college, some to active duty in the military services, but for many, there was nothing to go to—no home, no family, and no life. These few, including myself, would be faced with trials and tribulations that would destroy some of us.

Graduation day came. I looked to see if anyone would come, and as I expected, no one did. My brother couldn't get off duty. He did call, and I told him I had his picture under my gown, and it would be over my heart. My walk would be for the two of us. I looked for my forgotten parents, sisters, anyone who might claim me. This blessed event was one for my eyes alone. I was the first of my family to graduate from school, and in many ways, I was the first to complete anything!

As I looked at my classmates, those who had families and friends, I didn't feel sorry for myself. In fact, I was happy. I knew I'd come full circle in life. From the

103

time I was two, until now, I had been on my own. I had my brother with me always, and even though he wasn't here now, he was in spirit. I was proud of my accomplishments. I had truly beaten the odds. B.M. and Patty were there; however they were there for many of the other students as well. I'd broken my ties to them earlier, after my brother's last attack. It was my way of preparing myself for my next journey into life. I couldn't allow myself to depend on anyone. I could have, and I'm sure if I'd asked to stay with them they would have openly allowed me, but that wasn't my way. I had molded myself to go forward, with or without my brother. I knew I could do it. I'd already broken all sorts of odds getting this far, and had the scars to prove it!

We walked our final walk together, we laughed, we cried, and we spoke of the good and bad times each of us experienced. In the end, it was bittersweet. We all viewed this day as the beginning of a new day! Each of us knew it would be the last time we would ever see each other. We were going forth to start our lives in earnest. There would be some who wouldn't survive the summer, and some who would meet violent tragic deaths. Nothing was certain, as we filed out the auditorium doors. Our lives were changed forever, for better or for worse, by the events we experienced in this school.

Stark realization was thrust upon us as we concluded our graduation exercises. For those who weren't taken away by family or friends after the ceremonies, the remaining ones were gathered together by the state authorities—namely our counselors—and given one last message. We were told we were no longer wards of the State of Tennessee. It was no longer the responsibility of the state to fulfill our needs. We were quietly and firmly told we had eight hours to vacate the campus, or we would be escorted off. For many of those who remained, this was a shock. The message shook every fiber in their hearts and bodies. For some it scared the living hell out of them! They didn't know what to do, and many didn't have anywhere to turn. Some didn't have the foresight to prepare for this day, and they never saw it coming. To propose this message to teenagers who are alone in life is something I view as cold as death. Some in that meeting didn't last the summer. Some committed suicide; they weren't strong enough or equipped properly to handle what life threw at them. They surrendered to the tribulations of the world, giving up to something they weren't prepared to endure.

I was ready and looking forward! I wasn't excited, but I accepted the challenge with open arms, and I knew I could once again count on only one person in life—myself! My brother was in the military, and he couldn't be here to bail me out should I stumble and fall. I knew I would make mistakes; however I always knew the road I chose some fifteen years earlier had begun to prepare me for what lay ahead. I wasn't the best, smartest, or most resourceful; however I knew if I applied everything I had learned I would be okay. I had to keep my eyes open and look forward to each day as a new awakening, and learn the lessons of life as they were delivered. I'd broken every rule in the book—this shouldn't be happening— I knew I was at this crossroads simply because it was against all odds, something I've had expressed to me many times in my life.

As I look back on our lives, I realize we weren't properly equipped to go forth into the world and face the many responsibilities we would soon face! We were taught the curriculum that was required by the state; however we lacked an introduction into a world we knew nothing about. Many of us would soon come face to face with obstacles that would seem insurmountable! It wasn't that we weren't knowledgeable or tolerant of things of the world. We were, however we weren't skilled with insight into how the world worked and how it revolved. The changes we would be required to make in a short period of time were nothing short of dramatic. If anything, I believe we should've been informed as to what would be required of us once we entered the mainstream of life.

In many ways we were as hatchlings introduced to the world as prey that could be devoured at every turn. All we had to do was fall or trip, and the wolves of life would surely be on us in a fury! I found this myself out on many occasions!

The only difference between me and those who failed was that I prepared myself many years earlier. I knew many of the risks, and my eyes were open to the perils of life. This is not to say I wouldn't meet harm. I did, more than I care to remember, but when I did, I knew I had to regroup, move on quickly, try not to bleed much, and to learn from my mistakes. For many of my former classmates this wasn't the case, and they were soon devoured and destroyed by life. When we were discharged into the world, we didn't have anyone to lean on or to go to if we ran into harm's way! We were on our own to live and survive. It wasn't the state's responsibility any longer to give us insight or answer the many questions we had. Sink or swim is what many of us were allowed to do, and in many ways, we did just that!

I'm fortunate that I survived. I'm also pleased to inform you there are others who survived as I did. However, for those few who survived, there were several others who didn't. For these unfortunate ones, I'm truly sorry. I loved each of them dearly, as if they were my own family. In many ways they were—we lived as family in an environment that didn't tolerate weakness. We loved, cried, and laughed about many aspects of life. Now, however, no one laughed!

Today, our classmates hold reunions each year, and they reminisce about things we went through during our time on campus, and the trials and tribulations we faced. I haven't been to one of these reunions as of this date. It is my hope that when I do, I will be able to bring along this book as a living testament to the sacrifices we endured in our lives, and to awaken those who take for granted what family life means to them.

I am one voice who speaks for many. If my story is allowed to be told, perhaps it will make the journey easier for those who follow in our footsteps. This isn't to say I envy those who enter institutions as we did. It is only to enlighten those who teach and direct these dear and wonderful children, and perhaps enrich their lives with the necessary skills required for life we should've been given.

Finally, for those individuals from my school who didn't succeed, my wish is for them to know they are neither forgotten nor unloved. I remember them, and I'll never forget the many faces of those who enriched my life. It is because of them, and the experiences we shared, good and bad, that I succeeded. To each of them, I owe a debt of gratitude I can never begin to repay. Perhaps by writing this book I might be able to open a few eyes to our experience!

CHAPTER 13

Many years have passed since those troubled days of my youth. I've tried to keep in touch with many of my former classmates; however distance, business, and time have placed barriers that I've found insurmountable. As for my brother and I, how did we manage? Did we find success and fortune? Hardly, we've had our problems, much as any normal person would have. Each of us has gone his own way in life. We try to keep in touch; however our past has caused us to remain somewhat distant. Our lives have taken us in different directions; however one thing has always remained constant for us. We have always been there for each other, whenever the need required us to be there! If he needed me for anything, I was there for him, and he for me. Incredibly, we each married sisters, not once but twice! Our first marriages didn't last, but our second marriages lasted over twenty-five years.

Today my brother is a Chief Information Officer for a major company in California. He has worked in the computer industry for over twenty-five years and it has served him well. Is he happy? When we talk, he says he's fine; however I know his demons and his past haunt him to this day! He's ill as I write this last chapter and his days are numbered. I wanted to get my story out to him, to let him know how much I love him, and to let him know I didn't forget his pain and sorrow! Hopefully life will not leave him before he reads our story. In many ways, I believe he would be proud of me as I am of him.

As for me, I found my life in construction. I've worked eighteen years in the trenches, then went to the office to manage and estimate projects. I've been successful in my own right, though not as much as my brother. One thing I did learn along the way was to laugh at life and the events that structure my world each day. I try to take nothing for granted and always look upon the positives that make up my world. Today I work for an estimating department of a construction management company in Washington D.C. I'm presently by myself, divorced, as my brother has been, however happy and content with who I am and what I've become.

I look out my bedroom window when I awake each morning and thank God I'm alive! I don't have much in life, but I have something more precious than money or gold. Something no one can take from me. I have the knowledge that I've come from an era in life very few have walked or experienced. My brother and I succeeded where others failed, simply because we knew no other way to go through life.

My brother and I walked through life, two children with no one to lean on. We didn't feel sorry for ourselves, nor did we take anything for granted! Hard work paved the way for us. We each made mistakes along the way; however we learned quickly how to overcome. Feeling sorry for ourselves wasn't in our rule book—we both had a burning desire to prove others wrong in life, especially those who told us we wouldn't ever amount to anything.

We present living proof that anyone can succeed, if they have the will and guts to approach life with a perspective that they can succeed. My brother and I didn't have parents who were willing to structure us properly and forge our lives with this burning desire. We didn't need them. We had each other, and there wasn't anything we wouldn't do or sacrifice to help us grow.

SUMMARY

With everything I've endured in life, I've constantly struggled with this belief—There are children everywhere, who go to bed each night with no one reading to them, kissing them good night, or telling them they are loved and wanted! This is wrong. It is unconscionable and deplorable that we, the greatest country on the face of the earth, allow this to happen. If you look to the misfortunate in our world, and ask what is wrong, you only need to look and point to these simple facts. When you allow a child to grow and develop in an environment where there isn't love, nurturing, or caring, a child will resort to life as they are accustomed. If it's a world of abuse, neglect, hurt, and sorrow, then expect these children to use these resources in the next level of their lives and share them with their children. Anyone who is intelligent can expect the levels of suicide, abuse, crime, and indifference to excel in paramount order.

Children are our greatest joy in life. They are to be loved and cared for. If not, why should the world expect them to be any different from the environment they are raised within? It is my intent to open others' eyes to the injustice that exists within many of our child welfare services facilities today.

In the days of my youth, these facilities weren't prepared or structured to develop children properly for service into the world we know today. They weren't governed with structured programs to develop them positively. I shudder to think about enduring my journey again in life, with the different trials and tribulations that exist today. My brother and I suffered immensely through something we weren't prepared for. We weren't brought into this world to be slapped, beaten, abused, or neglected as others saw fit. We were miracles of life, as every child and adult who walks the face of the earth today is. The only differences in our lives was that the individuals responsible for giving us life were gutless and irresponsible. In preparing to write this book, I discovered other individuals who have experienced the same abuse and neglect in their lives will pass this on to their children, because it is inherently bred into their mentality. For my brother and I, this wasn't the case. We were raised within the confines of the state. It was their responsibility to structure and develop children who were placed in their care. It was their responsibility to give them an education, and to allow them a proper fighting chance to survive. In many examples I saw throughout my life, this wasn't the case. My story is about circumstances within my life and countless other children who lived and walked down the same path I had. There were many children who didn't survive, some at the hands of those who were assigned to develop and protect us for life.

My story is for those who survived their childhood as I have, and also for those who didn't. My objective is to let those who didn't survive know they aren't forgotten. To let them know, I remember their cries, their screams, and their tears! I remember the countless ambulances that took many of my former friends away from me. I remember holding many of them as they cried at night, afraid of potential attacks, afraid to close their eyes, knowing what might come any moment. I remember discussions with girls telling me about the abuse and neglect in their lives, from parents, family, and then counselors who were assigned to protect them. I remember someone I once loved, being taken from me by this same evil. I remember only too well the misfortune that found its way into my brother's life and mine, the many beatings, abuse, and downright torture!

This book is for everyone who can recognize and acknowledge that similar events and moments have happened within their lives. When you read these words, you can know you aren't alone and are truly special in life. Don't be afraid to let others know the hurt you experienced. My voice, as well as yours, will be heard if we speak and do not allow ourselves to be silenced. There are those who will discredit my words. Should they dare, they should be prepared for the truth. Let them dare to actively present their case in a world, in a country, who holds to the belief that we are to be loved and treated equal with respect and truth.

I hold to the belief that should anyone challenge the content of my words and my experiences, I will present to them not only scars and proof, I will present others, children like myself, who will gladly stand beside me, to let everyone hear our story, and the injustice we experienced. My words are spoken of true heart-wrenching events. These events have traveled with me throughout my life. I am shedding them now and walking away; I wish to carry them no longer.

Finally, to those who've harmed me and countless others in my lifetime, if you read my story, I want you to know I forgive you! You didn't know any better. Last of all, I want you to know that I beat you, I won, and I'm finally free!!!

110